PRAISE FOR *THROUGH TH*

"I will never forget meeting Pastor Levi over this past summer and hearing the incredible story of Lenya as we sat by the side of her grave. That experience, combined with this book, has impacted my life deeply, and I'm excited to share it with others."

—Kevin Durant

2014 NBA Most Valuable Player

"I'd give anything for Levi not to write this story. I'd rather he write a book about angels or Old Testament characters or the best way to pastor a church. If he wrote those books, that would mean he didn't have to write this one. And that would mean that his precious Lenya would be alive on earth. But she is in heaven. And he has this story. And he has told it well. With candor. With honesty. With hope. Maybe you need to hear it. No one gets though life unscathed. If you find yourself in a sad season, this story is for you."

—Max Lucado

Pastor and *New York Times* bestselling author of *Before Amen*

"This is one of the most powerfully transparent books I have ever read. If you are walking in a dark place and struggle to find words for your pain, Levi has them here. But there's more. There's hope—real hope, not wishful thinking. It's something only God can do. He can take the very thing that you knew would break you and make you stronger. This is a book we all need to read."

—Sheila Walsh

Speaker, Bible teacher, and bestselling author of *5 Minutes With Jesus*

"We cannot avoid loss regardless of our beliefs, our social status, or our affiliations. Most of us are not equipped to deal with it. Levi has framed up some practical thoughts and shares some experiences that can help us not only to cope with the pain of loss but to learn from it and thrive as a result. Sometimes tragic pain can help contribute to a life filled with greater purpose."

—Bob Hurley

Chairman and founder, Hurley LLC

"If you are hurting or struggling or have suffered a loss, please read *Through the Eyes of a Lion*, because there is hope. Unfortunately, during hardships so many people turn away from God. Levi's gut-wrenching account of losing his young daughter will draw you to the unconditional love of a heavenly Father who will comfort you when you hurt and give you his peace in your deepest pain."

—Craig Groeschel
Senior pastor, LifeChurch.tv
Author of *From This Day Forward: Five Commitments to Fail-Proof Your Marriage*

"Your heart will break as your read how [Levi's] faith was tested in so many ways. But your heart will soar as you read of how God has been faithful to the Luskos, and how they refuse to 'waste their pain.' . . . Because of Levi's razor sharp wit, *Through the Eyes of a Lion* will make you laugh out loud . . . and perhaps cry out loud as well . . . But you will be moved and helped to face whatever challenges come your way in life with faith in Jesus Christ as modeled by Levi and Jennie Lusko."

—Greg Laurie
Author and senior pastor,
Harvest Christian Fellowship

"Levi Lusko is a remarkable man. Despite having been through some of the most traumatic experiences anyone can have in this life, he has written a book that overflows with faith and hope. His heartrending insights are used to illustrate that suffering is not an obstacle to being used by God but an opportunity to be used by him all the more. This book will definitely help hurting people, regardless of what has been taken from them in this life—a marriage, a loved one, or a career—but it is also a book for everyone looking for a whole new way of living."

—Nicky Gumbel
Vicar of HTB in London
Pioneer of Alpha

"I don't think I've ever physically cried reading a book until this one. I read the whole thing on a flight from Seattle to Boston and couldn't put it down. Levi and Jennie's story is blazing with grace, and I was reminded that our hope as Jesus followers is a real, weighty, anchor-type hope, and that can change a life and the world."

—Jefferson Bethke

Author of the *New York Times* bestseller

Jesus > Religion

"If I had to create a hypothetical situation that would result in me *quitting* and *giving up*, it would be what Levi actually lived through. And not only did he 'live through it'—he's bringing new life to many by using a heart-breaking circumstance to teach people how to walk closer with Jesus. This is a book that will help everybody, in every walk of life."

—Carl Lentz

Pastor, Hillsong NYC

"This book hits the heart in many ways. It shows through Scripture that you can get through anything during hard times and the good times. There are parts that make you cry of sadness and of joy. The Lusko family goes through something no one should have to face, but though-out the book [Levi] shows how great God is. No matter what you're going through, he has a great plan for you . . . Everything is possible through God and only God! This book will change your life!"

—Matt Triplett

Professional bull rider

"I truly think this is going to be an incredibly significant book . . . The way [Levi] handles such a tragic subject is raw and real. He doesn't put any sugar coating on the journey the Lord has taken him through . . . The style in which he communicates is so rare and brilliant. The reader can actually hear his heart, like he's right there talking to them. . . . It's like injecting an adrenaline shot to live a life that runs toward trials, instead of away from them, for the sake of those who are in such desperate need of salvation, and for the sake of a kingdom that is to come. I'm certain Lenya's story is going to have a huge impact on those who read it."

—Dr. KP Yohannan

Founder and international director,

Gospel for Asia

"Levi's story is deeply moving and greatly inspiring. All at once it is heartbreaking and hopeful. Painful and powerful. When you leave this book, you will be a different person than when you came in."

—Phil Wickham
Recording artist

"Hearing Lenya Lion's story firsthand from Levi in Montana brought tears to my eyes, chills through my body, and most importantly, hope for my own family tragedy suffered. As a father of three children, I will never be able to put a measurement on how much impact the Lusko family has had in our lives. My prayer is that this book blesses you and anyone you share it with!"

—Adam Harrington
Assistant Coach, Oklahoma City Thunder
Founder, JEHH Memorial Fund

"Levi Lusko is a relatable leader and honest communicator to an emerging generation of young adults often characterized as distracted and hungry for purpose. A generation that doesn't believe leaders with real character still exist and a generation that believes encouraging words are often just patronizing or manipulative. *Through the Eyes of a Lion* is an urgent and raw memoir that is equally as relatable as it is actionable and edifying."

—Shea Parton
CEO, Apolis Global

"When Levi preached the message of this book to our crowded central London church, the effect was electric. He writes as he speaks: with the searingly raw intimacy of a parent and restrained reflection of a pastor on what has to be the most painful experience a father can go through. This book is powerful, authentic, deeply moving, and filled with hope. Read this book now. And keep it by your side for when you need to navigate the unexpected rough waters of life.

"Not many have looked into the eyes of a lion in the wild. I have. And I can see in my friend Levi the courage and determination of a lion though every page of this book."

—Ken Costa
Chairman, Alpha International

"Levi Lusko started to run toward the roar early in life. We witnessed his bold, brash faith unleashed on our youth group empowering teens to out-run sin. We owe the strength of our son's overcoming faith to Levi's fierce influence. Young men, husbands, fathers—this is the call to outrageous Christianity you've been craving."

—Lenya Heitzig
Director, she Ministries

"Levi Lusko brings a compelling message of hope to a generation lost in brokenness and pain. Very few people I have known have lived with such courageous faith as this man and his wife, Jennie, who experienced the worst and discovered God's grace and power to persevere. *Through the Eyes of a Lion* is a challenging call to triumphant faith and abundant life. This book will enable you and equip you to live with a lion's heart and an eternal purpose."

—Jack Graham
Pastor, Prestonwood Baptist Church

"Levi Lusko . . . not only challenges me to seek out a deeper, more meaningful relationship with Jesus, but through his faith stirs in me a passion to lead a life filled with uninhibited boldness and unrelenting courage. His story and message has encouraged me that there's even more in store for my life—more than just World Cup and Olympic victories. He invites me alongside him to use the loss of my own sister as a microphone to fulfill God's calling and ultimately his purpose for my life."

—Jillian Lloyden
Goalkeeper, US Women's National Soccer Team
Founder/director, The Keeper Institute

"The greatest ministry comes from the deepest agony. There is no worse day for a couple than the day they bury their baby girl. But, through that painful loss the Luskos have been carried by Jesus and trained in the school of suffering. This book is a hopeful, helpful, and healing map for others who are walking through the valley of the shadow of death."

—Mark Driscoll
Pastor

"*Through the Eyes of a Lion* isn't just about seeing the world around you. It's a powerful challenge to rely on God—completely and passionately—so you can discover a vision that goes far beyond what any eye can perceive. Because seeing life for what it really is isn't just about sight; it's about discovering, embracing, and experiencing God's vision for your life."

—Ed Young
Pastor, Fellowship Church
Author of *You! A Journey to the Center of Your Worth*

"Pain is the great equalizer. No one, whether forgotten or famous, preteen or preacher, escapes its tentacles. The question is, how will you face it? Pain gripped Levi and Jennie Lusko when Lenya, their precocious daughter, died suddenly of an asthma attack. But pain unspeakable made this family unstoppable. How? Levi hides none of his grief while making known the ways he broke free from pain's chokehold in this triumphant book."

—Skip Heitzig
Author and senior pastor of Calvary Albuquerque

"If you have ever feared that unspeakable loss and heartbreak would destroy your faith, fear no more! Levi Lusko opens his life and grief to us and lets us see God's mercy and beauty through the eyes of a Lion. Read and be radically altered forever."

—James MacDonald
Pastor, Harvest Bible Chapel
Author of *Vertical Church*

"I have never, in my childhood nor adulthood, had to endure a tragedy that involved massive pain. This fact in no way kept me from absolutely devouring this book. The hope that drips off of every page lands then soaks into the center of your soul. Levi has provided the world with a mantra on hope, no matter the extent of your pain."

—Carlos Whittaker
Author of *Moment Maker*

"This book is a gripping and powerful retelling of the real-life events that surrounded the sudden departure of Lenya Avery Lusko to heaven. I witnessed Levi and Jennie walk through the unimaginable and yet saw them live out their faith in a way that I believe is going to help people.

"This book is just part of the legacy of Little Lenya Lion. The impact she left on this world in her five short years is greater than most people do in ten lifetimes."

—Pedro Garcia
Pastor, Calvary Kendall

"It's odd to refer to a tremendous tragedy as being a source of extreme encouragement, but that's what happens through the background story of this incredible book. Levi is a skilled, transparent wordsmith, providing powerful perspective and relentless hope earned in the struggle of his own soul. I predict that this book will rock your world, and you'll recommend it as a '*must read*' the rest of your life!"

—Kevin Gerald
Lead pastor, Champions Centre

"This book is a prescription of real hope for the broken heart. No matter what season of life you are in, Levi speaks to the human condition with honesty, grace, and wisdom, reminding us all that in our weakness the power of God is truly faithful to sustain us. Levi allows his pain to become medicine for all of us, and I am so grateful for his transparency. This is a book you will read and share again and again."

—Rich Wilkerson Jr.
Pastor, Vous Church

"My dear friend Levi Lusko has penned down a beautiful portrait of life, death, God, and hope. I can't think of many people who can articulate their life experience like Levi can. But I also don't know of anyone who has embraced God, faced reality, and celebrated heaven better than Levi. I am moved by this book."

—Chad Veach
Pastor, Zoe Church

"The story of Fresh Life Church continues to defy the odds, and at the heart of the church's story is the triumph and pain of the Lusko family. Levi Lusko is a young gun, an up-and-coming voice you should listen to. This riveting book gives a glimpse into the heart-wrenching story of one family, but also a larger glimpse into and clear lenses for seeing the power and triumph of the kingdom of God. . . . It pumped fuel and oxygen into my spiritual veins! It's inspiring and a much-needed road map for high-octane living, regardless of what season you're in. You'll be laughing, crying, and shouting. Read this book!"

—Brad Lomenick

Former president and key visionary, Catalyst

Author of *H3 Leadership*

"Levi is one of a new generation of preachers that understands the importance of maintaining Biblical orthodoxy while putting the gospel forth in the current cultural context. Whether he's preaching or writing, his passion for both Jesus and souls comes across loud and clear."

—Brian Brodersen

Pastor, Calvary Chapel, Costa Mesa, California

"Solid in its Biblical perspective and so personal in its presentation. God will use *Through the Eyes of a Lion* to be strength and help for many people. Read it for yourself, and get this book into the hands of others."

—David Guzik

Pastor, Calvary Chapel Santa Barbara

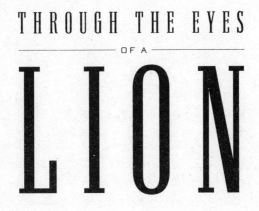

THROUGH THE EYES OF A LION

THROUGH THE EYES OF A LION

FACING IMPOSSIBLE PAIN
FINDING INCREDIBLE POWER

LEVI LUSKO

W PUBLISHING GROUP
AN IMPRINT OF THOMAS NELSON

Published in Nashville, Tennessee, by W Publishing Group, an imprint of Thomas Nelson.

Published in association with the literary agency of Wolgemuth & Associates, Inc.

Thomas Nelson titles may be purchased in bulk for educational, business, fund-raising, or sales promotional use. For information, please e-mail SpecialMarkets@ThomasNelson.com.

Library of Congress Cataloging-in-Publication Data

Lusko, Levi.
Through the eyes of a lion : facing impossible pain, finding incredible power / Levi Lusko.
pages cm
Includes bibliographical references.
ISBN 978-0-7180-3214-2 (trade paper)
1. Suffering--Religious aspects--Christianity. I. Title.
BV4909.L87 2015
248.8'6--dc23

2015009292

Printed in the United States of America

18 19 LSCC 18 17 16

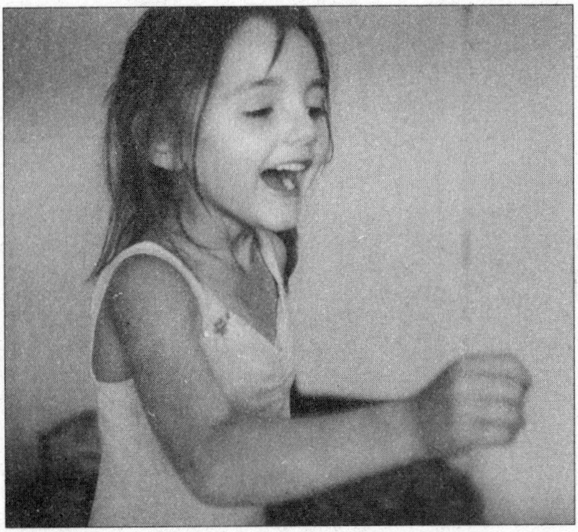

Photo: Kelli Trontel

For Lenya Avery Lusko

(aka Lenya Lion)

L. L. A. A. A. L. forever. Gangsters for life.

CONTENTS

FOREWORD

"Bro, you've gotta try it. Trust me, it's amazing."

Levi Lusko has said these words to me about stand-up paddle-boarding, alpine sliding, the scoop-neck tee at AllSaints, Olbas Oil, sriracha sauce, and the state of Montana. About all of these, he was right.

I don't know if I've ever met a more enthusiastic evangelist than Levi. For Jesus, obviously. But really, for anything he loves. And since he has proven to have excellent taste and judgment in . . . well, almost everything, I've learned to trust the instincts of my friend.

But when he first told me he wanted to write this book, I cringed. Not because I doubted his competence. The guy is a world-class wordsmith, whether he's in the pulpit or hanging out poolside. I had no doubt his signature blend of hard-charging application, pop culture cleverness, and endlessly likable personality would transfer to the page. I mean, who would have the guts or the giftedness to make a seamless spiritual connection between a Bible verse inscribed on a tombstone and Spider-Man? Levi Lusko, that's who.

No, I wasn't even a little bit worried about the finished product. I knew it would be powerful, profound, practical, and any other positive *P* words you can think of. (Sorry, preacher habit.) And *Through the Eyes of a Lion* didn't disappoint.

What I was concerned about was the price of the book. Not what you paid for it, but what Levi paid to write it. You'll understand by the time you've finished the first chapter that this book is worth exponentially more than whatever you invested in it. What it cost Levi and his wife, Jennie, to be able to share these truths, however, is impossible to calculate. I'm grateful they were willing.

I was privileged to witness the process that produced this message. The wisdom, encouragement, and inspiration you're about to receive came from Levi's heart the way precious oil comes from unripened olives: under extreme, almost unbearable pressure.

And considering the pain he's experienced, Levi could have written a book that dripped into the system like morphine, purely to provide a sensation of comfort. Instead, he has issued a manifesto to "adrenalize" your calling, without sacrificing a milliliter of comfort.

On the night of the events you'll read about in chapter 3, I spoke with Levi and Jennie on the phone for about ten minutes. What they said in those moments marked me for life. The way they have lived out what they said in those moments is the message of this book, and I believe it will tattoo you too.

Levi loves superheroes, and to me, he is one in real life. That's because he lives better than he preaches, and he's one of the best preachers I know.

This is more than a book. It's a lifeline. I believe in it. Levi has lived it. It is soul healing and world changing, concurrently.

And, might I add, in the spirit of Levi:

Bro/Sis, you've gotta *try it. Trust me, it's amazing.*

—Steven Furtick

Charlotte, North Carolina

INTRODUCTION

THE NAKED EYE

It is early morning, and I am walking along the waterfront in Seattle near the Pike Place Market. Bracing myself against the damp, chilly air, I zip my leather jacket up to my throat but still feel the wind cut daggers through me. I will them to run me through.

Clouds fill all of the visible sky—dark, menacing, and turbulent. My hands are burning. I start to run. Can I outrun this? I run until my legs burn too. The sky matches my soul. Seattle is a good place to be sad.

I will never walk her down the aisle.

She will never have a baby.

She lost only one tooth.

She will never read a chapter book.

Memories from only thirty days ago race past like floodwaters and sweep me off my feet. It's as though I am in an abandoned movie theater inside my mind, being forced to watch archival footage from a horror movie that is my life. Frame after frame clicks by: Looking into her beautiful brown eyes. Hearing the sound of her rich, raspy voice. Seeing her lie there on the counter. Little red socks. Emergency lights flashing in through the kitchen window. A waiting room. Snowflakes melting as they hit our tear-stained cheeks. Temperatures so cold they cause our fingers and ears to sting as we stand in a cemetery blanketed in white, everyone wearing dark peacoats. Staring at a small, white box. The sound of voices singing Chris Tomlin's "I Will Rise."

This can't be real.

These thoughts swim through my mind and try to strangle me. My heart is shattered into a thousand pieces, each shard jagged and razor sharp. The pain is surreal, deafening, and catastrophic. My eyes burn. I want to cry, but the tears won't come. I want to scream, but it won't help. I am afraid. But I'm not alone.

This is war.

⚓ ⚓ ⚓

Every moment of every day, you are in an invisible battle that ever rages on. As real as the ancient ones you read about in history class and as current as the clips shown on the evening news, it's as bloody as the French Revolution and as sinister as a suicide bombing. This is not something that could happen someday—it's happening right now. You've heard of the War of the Roses? This is the War of the Lenses.

Most of the time, we shuffle along quite oblivious to the great majority of what is actually happening. We drink our lattes and double-click our friends' pictures on Instagram, never giving thought to the fact that we are being watched. There are grades to get at school and money to make at work. Bills don't pay themselves. You probably need to organize the garage, don't you?

(I know I do. As much fun as it is having to channel my inner David Blaine to get out of my car, it would be marvelous to open my door more than ten inches.) All the while, unseen things all around us go unnoticed.

I eventually made it to where I was heading that day in Seattle: Starbucks. Not the one that is actually in the Pike Place Market and is the first store the company ever opened—the one just a block up the hill from it. The original one is cool to see at least once, if only just to marvel at the humble origins of a brand that has quite literally conquered the world, but not all Starbucks shops are created equal. Certain stores have Clover machines and serve a special Reserve menu of exotic beans from around the world. You can use the company's app to find these special locations. Even in pain I have standards. (Confession: I did name my youngest daughter Clover after the coffee machine.)

As I walked in, the vicious waves of sadness that had been slamming me onto the rocks and stealing my breath ever since I had left the hotel that morning subsided enough for me to compose myself. Outside the sky remained stormy, but inside me the downpour had been briefly suspended. I walked in and ordered, then sat down on a stool by the bar and waited for my coffee. I looked around and wondered if anyone knew how much I was hurting. Scanning the room, I saw many people but felt very, very alone. How many times had I sat next to people who were suffering but been completely unaware of the agony they were going through?

Nursing my black coffee, I pulled out my phone and navigated to an app that contained a selection of Bible verses to read in the morning and at night for each day of the year. A verse from Romans 3:22 caught my attention: "The righteousness of God, through faith in Jesus Christ, to all and on all who believe."

Feeling anything but full of faith, I chose to believe again. Right there on that stool, I took heart, shifting my weight onto God's shoulders. The prayer that followed wasn't pretty or put together; it was a text message from my gut that said I needed help: *Please fill me with your Spirit and give me strength right now. I believe.*

Big breath in. Big breath out.

I read a few more verses, then changed apps and dumped my thoughts into a note, venting my emotions and the things that had lit my mind on fire.

I left the cafe. Everything was the same as when I went in. Nothing was the same as when I went in. The details of my life hadn't changed, but I had. I had switched lenses, and so I saw things differently. I still saw what was there, but now that wasn't all I saw. I could see the invisible.

This is the war: every moment of every day, we must make the all-important choice of whether we will rely on the naked eye. Will we trust what we can see is there, or believe what God says is there? It's a decision we are continually confronted with. The apostle Paul put it this way: "So we don't look at the troubles we can see now; rather, we fix our gaze on things that cannot be seen. For the things we see now will soon be gone, but the things we cannot see will last forever" (2 Corinthians 4:18 NLT).

WILL WE TRUST WHAT WE CAN SEE IS THERE, OR BELIEVE WHAT GOD SAYS IS THERE?

Making the choice to see the invisible is not always as dramatic as it was that morning in Seattle. Sometimes it's far more low-key, and that's when it can be the most difficult. Trials have a way of splashing cold water on our faces and rousing us from sleep. It is much easier to slip into cruise control when the sun is out and the birds are chirping. For every person who has been destroyed by suffering, there are probably ten who have been wrecked by success. Trust me when I say this: the issue isn't whether your life is going well or falling apart; the question is, what makes you so sure you can tell the difference? Things are seldom as they appear.

PRESENT BUT NOT ALWAYS ACCOUNTED FOR

Gehazi needed glasses. Sorely outnumbered and about to die, he knew that he and his boss had just moments to live. At any minute the door would be kicked in and soldiers would spill in like ants through a crack to end their lives. If only he had taken that cruise on the Mediterranean. His life was over. Or was it?

Gehazi was the servant of a prophet named Elisha. Gehazi's master had been given X-Men-like superpowers by God that enabled him to hear from over a country away the things people whispered in their bedrooms. This made him dreadfully valuable to the king of Israel when it came to espionage and counterterrorism. He was an old-school version of a surveillance drone, except without the billion-dollar price tag. Elisha's uncanny knack for knowing what Israel's enemies were going to do before they themselves did also put a target on his back—and that of anyone close to him. His servant Gehazi, for instance. Collateral damage.

A bounty had been placed on Elisha's head. Vultures circled. That morning Gehazi opened the door and saw that they were surrounded. Soldiers fanned out around them as far as the eye could see. The BC equivalent of red laser sight beams appeared on his chest from every direction. This was it.

"Master!" he managed through clenched teeth, without moving an inch.

Elisha made his way to the doorway, casually glancing at the leering mob that had amassed and was slowly approaching from all four directions. Clearly unfazed, he asked Gehazi what was the matter.

Oh no, Gehazi thought. *He's finally lost it! What does he mean, "What's the matter?" Does he think they're here to sell us Girl Scout cookies?*

Gehazi gasped and then whispered, "These soldiers! What are we going to do?"

"Don't worry about it," Elisha said.

This was almost more than Gehazi could handle. Mind you, he had seen some things in his time as Elisha's assistant. But this was going to the next level. His master clearly was delusional. They had maybe five minutes before the soldiers reached them, and perhaps an additional two where they could hold them off if they wedged furniture behind the door—and that was the best-case scenario. Yet here was Elisha, practically singing the lyrics to "It's a Small World" and pretending everything was going to be all right. Things were most definitely not going to be all right.

Elisha continued: "There are more on our side than on the enemies'."

Gehazi processed this and did some quick counting. Looking at the soldiers, he estimated that there were five or six thousand. Then he looked at himself and Elisha, and the counting was much easier: one, two.

Good thing Elisha got into the ministry, because math is clearly not his strong suit, Gehazi thought, genuinely feeling sorry for the bald, weathered man who was obviously nuts.

Elisha smiled, and with a twinkle in his eye he prayed, "Lord, open his eyes so he can see."

Gehazi looked outside once more. He still saw the soldiers with their armor and their weapons, but now that wasn't *all* he saw. On the hills above those soldiers, he could now see another army—a bigger, far more powerful army. There were glorious, glowing warriors riding chariots that shimmered like fire, spilling up the canyon into the sky. Bright like the dawn and as powerful as a thunderous waterfall, each of them wielded a terrible bow with an arrow at the ready. There must have been a hundred thousand of them.

The sight made Gehazi's fingertips tingle and his heart flutter. He felt giddy like a child and wanted to laugh and run. Safe—above all else, he felt safe. And he was.

What is so important about this Bible story (2 Kings 6:15–17) is that the angels didn't show up when Gehazi's eyes were opened. They were there when he couldn't see them. Present but invisible. Gehazi was staring at them every time he looked outside; he just didn't know it. When God opened Gehazi's eyes to see the unseen, he still saw the enemy soldiers. They didn't go away. Why was he no longer afraid of them? He now understood that the thing that had him surrounded was itself surrounded by God.

So it always is.

HIDDEN IN PLAIN SIGHT

The best stargazing conditions are outside of town. On a cloudless, dark night, when you are far away from civilization, it is possible to see as many as five thousand stars. A place like Montana, for example—that's where I live, by the way—is a sweet place to stargaze. My wife, daughters, and I love to lie out on the driveway on clear summer nights and look up at the sky, especially when there are shooting stars to watch. A couple of summers ago, during the annual Perseid meteor shower, there were one hundred shooting stars per hour streaking across the sky, more than one a minute. Lenya and Alivia (my then four- and six-year-olds) and I snuggled up on a blanket on the lawn, oohing and aahing at the show.

In the city, all the light pollution keeps the visible number of stars down to only a couple hundred, even on the clearest of nights. Abraham wouldn't have needed too much faith to believe God's promises if he had been in New York City instead of Ur of the Chaldees when God called him, if you know what I mean. But what is important to remember is that even when you can't see the stars, they are still there.

Keep your place here in the book, and go look up at the sky. Go on. Do it. Don't just keep reading. I mean it. If you are outside, it's easy—just look up. If you are indoors, go to a window, or better yet, open a door.

What did you see? Any stars out there? It's daytime, you say? Ah. Sorry about that. But that works just as well, because you know that you were still looking at stars, right? No matter what time of day or night it is, there are always stars in the sky. Just because you can't see them doesn't mean they aren't there.

No matter whether you are in Manhattan looking at hundreds of stars, or in Montana seeing thousands, there are always more. Millions and millions and millions more. The human eye sees more than you realize—much more than you can actually process. For instance, when you look up at the stars, you are technically looking at all of them; you just can't perceive all you are seeing. I can prove it to you. A telescope or other lens just magnifies and brings into focus what you are already looking at, what is there all along. Even in the daytime, the stars are right in front of you, hidden in plain sight. The reason you can't make out what you are seeing is because of distance and interference.

So it is spiritually. You must not rely on the naked eye. What you think you see is not all that is there. There are unseen things. Spiritual things. Eternal things. You must learn to see life *through the eyes of a Lion.* Doing so is to utilize the telescope of faith, which will not only allow you to perceive the invisible—it will give you the strength to do the impossible.

ONE

DESTINED FOR IMPACT

A man named Daryl walked into a pawnshop in Los Angeles with a guitar. He popped the case and asked the clerk what he could get for it. When the inevitable haggling was over, he emerged with a fistful of cash. Two hundred fifty dollars, to be exact. Not exactly a jackpot. If the guitar had been a junker left over from lessons he had been forced to take as a child, that could even be considered decent money. But this was not some old beater, and $250 was nowhere close to decent money. This guitar belonged to Tom Petty and was worth eighty times what Daryl sold it for. He had been ripped off more than he could possibly imagine.

In addition to not being all that bright, Daryl was a thief. He worked as a security guard at a California soundstage, where Tom Petty and his world-famous Heartbreakers were rehearsing in preparation for a tour. One day the group discovered that five electric guitars were missing. Daryl was being paid to protect the gear in the facility, but it turned out the gear needed protection from him. The five guitars he stole were worth more than $100,000 combined.[1]

Perhaps Daryl was desperate for money, and so no price was too low. Or maybe he had no idea what the instrument was actually worth. That would be hard to believe, considering whom he stole it from. A quick Google search could have filled him in. But what I couldn't stop thinking about when I read the news story was this: when you don't recognize the value of what you have in your hands, you will always get from it far less than it is worth.

We're not talking about guitars anymore, are we? you might be thinking. No, we're talking about something much bigger: you. More specifically, the potential you carry deep down inside.

YOU ARE THE ONE, NEO

There is a calling on your life. A great, big, God-sized calling. God has plans for you and has been dreaming about them since before you were even born. You are destined for impact. My heart is racing just thinking about it! I wish I could jump out of this book, look you in the eyes, and tell you to your face so that you could see that I mean it. And then if you still didn't get it, I would shake your shoulders and say it louder. I pray that, by the time you reach the end of the book, God will have poured Red Bull into your veins and your heart will be pumping like a racehorse, because you'll be so eager to see your destiny fulfilled.

If you are reading these words, you have been given a unique, powerful, custom-built platform. A voice. As long as there is breath in your lungs, you have a microphone in your hands. There are things God intends for you to accomplish that no one else has been chosen for. Words he wants you to speak. Actions that speak louder than words. And through it all, he wants you to leave a mark, to put a dent in the universe.

But if you don't understand that calling, you will undervalue it. Just as a pawnshop employee seems to be doing you a favor by taking some "old piece of junk"—that is actually priceless—off your hands, a failure to understand how powerful and extraordinary God's plans for you are will lead to you being taken advantage of by the enemy and failing to live up to your potential.

I don't know what you see when you look in the mirror. If you are like me, there is a long list of things you wish you could change. The bags under my eyes say that I don't get enough sleep. My nose is crooked, as it has been since middle school, when I broke it jumping on a friend's trampoline. I'd like to think it gives me character in an Owen Wilson kind of way, but most of the time I just see that it's not straight. Though I am only thirty-two, I already see little lines forming near the corners of my eyes that speak of the aging process that has already begun. When I first wake up most mornings, I splash water on my face, look at myself, and think, *Dude, you look like you got hit by a truck*. But lately there have been a lot of times when I have seen a sadness in my face that hasn't always been there.

Regardless of what you see looking back at you while you brush your teeth, I can tell you with zero hesitation that to God there is nothing ordinary about you. You spit your toothpaste out just like everybody else, but the truth is, you are complex, special, and one of a kind. I realize I'm getting all Barney the Purple Dinosaur on you, but I'm dead serious. There is nothing even remotely close to normal about you.

The trouble with this sort of talk is that callings are invisible.

You can't see destiny. It's not readily apparent when you look at it with the naked eye. If you take a selfie, you won't see the version of yourself you are meant to become, no matter what filter you use.

> IF YOU TAKE A SELFIE, YOU WON'T SEE THE VERSION OF YOURSELF YOU ARE MEANT TO BECOME, NO MATTER WHAT FILTER YOU USE.

YOU MATTER MORE THAN YOU KNOW

To make things worse, just about every part of our lives makes us feel as though we are just another number, just another person. A cog in the machinery of the universe. A little lemming.

There is perhaps no experience in life that makes you feel less special than being at the division of motor vehicles, trying to obtain or renew your driver's license. Take a number, sit down, and lose a little bit of your soul. We will call you sometime this decade. Maybe.

Even the sign at McDonald's makes you feel insignificant: You are just one out of a gazillion people who have eaten a Big Mac. Give us your money. We can't even get fat without being made to feel like a tiny statistic.

Recently I bumped my head and cut my scalp just to the right of my part. The laceration was about an inch and a half long. I had been leaning over below an open window, and when I stood up the corner tore into my head. The people I was with took one look at me and said, "You need to go to the ER."

The place was packed. People everywhere. You'd think a bleeding head wound would get me to the front of the queue. No such luck. The receptionist told me it would be an hour and a half. Four and a half hours later, a frazzled nurse finally called me back.

"Levy Loose Co," she said, completely butchering my name as countless people have over the years. (For the record, my first name is pronounced Levi, just like the jeans, and *Lusko* is pronounced Ləskō, and yes, I did have to use Google to figure out that an upside-down *e* is how you make the *uh* sound.) Completely out of dignity, I didn't even bother to correct her. I walked in her direction, holding gauze to my head, and said, "I'm Levy Loose Co. Please fix my head." Half a bottle of superglue later, I was on my way. (You read that right. They actually glued my head shut.)

So much of our lives feels pretty unimportant, composed of activity that is seemingly insignificant. Folding clothes, writing papers, paying bills, watching *Seinfeld* reruns, eating dinner. Repeat. But don't let the simplicity of life fool you. You are so close to the details that it can be difficult to get perspective, but you are a part of a much larger story. You matter more than you know.

You might feel pretty ordinary or average. Perhaps you even have the Cs on your report card to prove it. If you were a late bloomer like me, middle school was brutal for you. Have you been picked on or squashed down by people? That gets old pretty quickly and eventually can cause you to believe what is being said about you. Even worse, maybe you have been flat-out told you are worthless. You feel tempted to accept that you are doomed to alcoholism, like your father before you, or divorce, like just about everyone you know. Hear me loud and clear: these are all lies!

You were made in the image of God. That's right, made. You are not smart mud or a monkey wearing pants. God *made* you. Fearfully, wonderfully, he knit you together inside your mother. You're no accident. Out of all creation, God made humans, male and female, to be like him. And as his image-bearer, you possess a gift no animal was given—self-awareness. You have free will. You are not a robot or a puppet.

Like God, you have a personality. A sense of humor. You can laugh and sing, make love and create, dream and destroy. You have feelings and can be hurt. When things don't go our way, we get sad and can be grieved, just like God. This might surprise you, but God doesn't always get what he wants, and neither do we. Jesus knocks at the doors of our hearts, and we have to invite him inside in order to be saved. He is a gentleman, so he knocks. He won't go all SEAL Team Six and kick the door down. He gives us the dignity and responsibility of making our own decisions.

You are also immortal. The question is not whether you will live forever, but where. Four hundred years from now, and four thousand years after that, you will still exist—you will still be alive, and you will still be you.

Then there is the matter of what God was willing to spend to redeem you and give you hope, when sin and death had their suffocating stranglehold on your life. The value of something comes from what someone is willing to pay to have it. And boy, were you expensive. The Bible says that while we were dead in our sins, God demonstrated his love for us by sending his Son to die for us (Romans 5:8). You weren't purchased with any common currency, like gold or silver, but with the precious blood of Jesus. His veins were opened, and then, hanging on two pieces of wood on top of a hill shaped like a skull, the Son of God died to pay the price for every wrong thing you have done. Sin is a capital crime, so he died to set you free.

There is no higher price that has ever been paid for anything in history. No Rolex, luxury yacht, penthouse apartment, work of art, or private island can come close to being as outrageously expensive as the price Jesus paid to secure your release from captivity. When he was faced with the thought of you being separated from him and the plans he has for your life, he gladly strapped himself into your electric chair and died in your place so you could go free. You are valuable—not just by birth, but because blood was spilled so you could be born again.

That's not all. As a child of God you have been entrusted with the Holy Spirit. The same Holy Spirit that raised Jesus from the dead now lives in your heart and is ready and waiting to be activated. Greater energy courses through you than can be measured with horsepower. As often as you ask, the Spirit is prepared to surge afresh into your soul, like the power coming from Iron Man's glowing chest piece, turbocharging your efforts as you rise up to do all God wants you to do.

Then there are the gifts and unique privileges you have been given. There are spiritual capabilities and also skills, talents, and abilities. He has made you passionate about certain things. You have specific connections and opportunities that I haven't been given. There are people you get to talk to every day whom it would take a miracle for a preacher to get in front of. But for you it's as effortless as sitting in second period or clocking in for an afternoon shift at your job. Lucky!

Oh, and you have also been tasked with the greatest mission that has ever been undertaken in the history of the world—the Great Commission, a mission to go fishing. The orders from your commanding officer are pretty clear: go into all the world and preach the gospel to every creature. People who believe will be saved, but if they do not, they are not. You're pretty much like Frodo, except instead of a ring that has to get to the volcano, you have a message that is the only hope of saving mankind from sin and death.

ROYAL REPRESENTATIVES AND SPIRITUAL SUPERHEROES

So let's recap: The God who created the universe made you and trusted you with his image. The most important person ever to live was willing to die to save you. You are tapped into a power source greater than the electricity generated at Niagara Falls added to the mushroom cloud of Hiroshima, plus you have spiritual superpowers. If I were tweeting about you, I would hashtag it this way: #NoBigDeal #ReallyBigDeal #TheFirstHashtagWasSarcastic.

I hope you are starting to get a sense of how incredibly, wildly unordinary you are. You, my friend, were put on this earth to make waves, disrupt the status quo, and kick over some stinking applecarts. The apostle Peter said that you are "a chosen generation, a royal priesthood, a holy nation," God's "own special people" that he brought "out of darkness into His marvelous light" so you might proclaim his praises (1 Peter 2:9). *Hello?!* Look at those adjectives! I mean, I could go off on the nouns, but even just glancing at the descriptive words should give you a sense of how God sees you: *chosen, holy, special, marvelous,* and *royal.*

I have been in the presence of royalty only once. I was about ten feet from Prince William, Prince Harry, and Kate Middleton, the duchess of Cambridge, at a bike race I attended in England. I rode to the race on my bicycle, traveling about seventy-five kilometers from York, where I was staying. They flew in their royal helicopter to see it. I had to fight through the crowds of

200,000-plus people to get to a friend of mine, who had gotten up at the crack of dawn to save us a spot by the winner's podium. They were escorted through us common people to their private box to see the racers go by, arriving just moments before the action started, while the rest of us stood for hours, packed in like sardines. They were given the royal treatment. Why? Because they are royalty. A day is coming when one of those two brothers will sit as king on the throne of England.

That's earthly royalty. You are a part of the royal line of heaven—kings and priests to our God. Citizens of a coming kingdom that can't be shaken. No, you don't have a tiara or a crown yet, but you are a son or daughter of the King who's higher than all other kings! There is no game when it comes to his throne. He shall reign forever and us with him. To use an epic line from the movie *The Avengers*, "You are burdened with glorious purpose."[2]

Knowing what I know about you, I am humbled by the chance to write something you would read. Far better than cutting in line or owning a ceremonial sword (though let's be honest: that would be pretty sweet), the privilege attached to our status as Christ followers is that we get to represent God. That's what it means to be an ambassador. You are a royal representative of the crown. And we are deputized, on behalf of the King, to offer pardons and full-fledged citizenship to any and all who will receive it. That's heavy stuff!

Your potential is unlimited. God's desire is to do through your life "exceedingly abundantly above" what you could ask for or even think of (Ephesians 3:20). Whether you are sixteen or sixty, no matter where you have been or what you have seen, you haven't even scratched the surface of all that God intends for you. There is music inside you waiting to burst out, poems you're meant to write, horses you're meant to ride, people you're meant to touch, companies waiting to be launched, things you're supposed to invent, clothing lines you'll design—all to the glory of God.

"But what about the laundry? The bills? The fact that I still need to go to the DMV and I literally ate a Big Mac for lunch today?" you ask.

I have told you that you are a spiritual superhero, a part of the royal family that will reign through all eternity. But day to day your life is made up of seconds and minutes that often don't feel all that special. How do you live out an extraordinary calling while doing ordinary things and living in a world that is all screwed up?

HOW DO YOU LIVE OUT AN EXTRAORDINARY CALLING WHILE DOING ORDINARY THINGS AND LIVING IN A WORLD THAT IS ALL SCREWED UP?

That is not only the million-dollar question; it is why we desperately need to have our eyes opened up. Living out the calling on your life isn't necessarily going to mean doing entirely new things, but doing things in an entirely new way. You have to see your life through the eyes of a Lion.

I had my pupils dilated the last time I was in for an eye exam. I protested and complained and begged the doctor not to do it. He insisted and promised me I would get a sucker if I would behave. When your pupils are dilated, it makes you extremely farsighted. It's an unsettling procedure that allows extra light to come into your eyes so that you can see things far away in great detail, but things close up are blurry and out of focus. I can't stand that feeling and couldn't wait for my pupils to shrink back to normal so that I could get on with my life.

I kept getting so frustrated while I waited for the dilation to wear off, because I was unable to make out anything on my phone. It was all blurry. I finally figured out that if I held my phone at arm's length, I was able to read it. You should have seen my wife laughing at me holding my phone several feet away from my face. But I didn't care. I was back in the game.

My aim is for God to use this book to dilate the eyes of your soul so that you will see things as laser sharp that are yet far off, and so that all the things that seem so real, but are not going to last, would lose their crispness. I want to show you that God doesn't expect you to be happy about what has been torn from your hands—whether it's a marriage, your health, a job, or someone you love—but if you are willing to trust him, he can turn trash into triumph.

TWO

COWS DIE THERE

In the infuriating kids' show *Dora the Explorer,* Dora has a magic map that springs out of her evil little backpack to help her whenever she gets lost. All she has to say is, *"Map!"* Then she tells the kids watching at home to say it louder. (The show is interactive so that the kids will remain glued to it while Mom desperately tries to get a shower, pay bills, or—in less productive moments—scroll through her feed on Instagram.) Map comes out singing, ready to help Dora and her friend Boots—a monkey who wears shoes but no clothes (#Hmmm #NoComment)—get to wherever it is they need to be.

What I have discovered in the years I've been a Christian is that there is no magic map for navigating your way to the epic life God has called you to. Even if you were to say it louder, there would be no secret source to tell you, for instance, what state you should live in or what college to apply to.

But Levi, you might be thinking, *there is a magic map. It's called the Word of God! Hello?! Aren't you, like, a pastor? How can you not know this? It even has a theme song: "The B-I-B-L-E! Yes, that's the book for me! I stand alone on the Word of God, the B-I-B-L-E!" Don't you know that we're supposed to turn to Scripture as a map?*

I agree with you—to a certain extent. The Bible is without a doubt meant to function as a GPS unit for the soul and is there to set the pace for our lives. Proverbs 6:22 tells us that when we roam, God's words will lead us; when we sleep, they will keep us; and when we awake, they will speak with us. Jesus said that the Holy Spirit would bring to mind things we have read and heard from the Scriptures at key moments to keep us pointed in the right direction.

But I've discovered that sometimes what we need to do isn't clear; sometimes it's confusing. Sometimes there is more than one good option. And nowhere are we told in Scripture that we will never feel lost. In fact, just the opposite: Scripture is full of tension. People are put in situations where they are kept out of the loop and left to wriggle a bit, like a fish on a hook. Think of Job during the difficult middle of his story. He lost everything. Why? Because he was in sin? No, because he was in the will of God. His trial came because God was bragging about him to the devil. But remember, Job was unaware of all of this. He had never read the book of Job.

The Bible doesn't have a chapter and verse for every decision you have to make. Take dating, for example. There are verses that will tell you what kind of spouse to look for, what kind of character the person you date should have (2 Corinthians 6:14, Proverbs 31, and so on). And the Bible tells you clearly what sexual activities are out of bounds before you are married (Ephesians 5:3). God has a whole lot to say about navigating the treacherous waters that are your love life. But what the Bible *doesn't* tell you is which one to pick if you have found two candidates that both fit the bill. Look all you want, but there is no chapter and verse for blonde or brunette.

Scripture will tell you not to punch your boss in the head when he acts like a jerk (Matthew 5:39). But the Bible doesn't tell you what to do when he offers you a promotion that comes with longer hours. You will have to carefully decide which is better for your family—more money or more of you.

When you are in the middle of these kinds of confusing situations, it is hard to get a sense of whether you are moving in the right direction—or if you are even moving at all. And though the Bible gives us the principles we need to live a life that honors God, it is no magic map. If it were, there would be no need for faith. There would be no need for God. You might feel lost or confused about where you are supposed to go or what you are supposed to do, but I challenge you to see that as a necessary part of the process.

LEVI'S GENES

Ever since I was young, I've known I was going to be a pastor. It wasn't so much that I wanted to be one or that I thought it would be fun; I just had the impression that it was what was supposed to happen. There was a brief stint around age four where I told my parents I was going to be a baker so I could eat all the cookies I baked. But I suspect that had more to do with the fact that my parents were health-food nuts who allowed us to have chocolate milk instead of white milk only on our birthdays. For treats we were given nasty candies made with carob. They were terrible. Whenever I got the chance, I would sneak junk food, and my dreams were full of sugary cereals like Fruity Pebbles and Golden Grahams. (Not Cap'n Crunch, though. Even in my dream life I didn't want the roof of my mouth to get beaten up.) When I grew up, I discovered that the prodigal son in the Bible parable, when he lost all his money and lived with the pigs, tried to eat the indigestible carob pods they were fed. My parents had been feeding me swine candy!

The bakery dream was short-lived, though. By kindergarten I had shaken it off and would tell people I was going to be a pastor, just like my dad. His name is Chip, and I earned the nickname "Microchip" because of the way I tried to dress like him and followed him around church on Sundays.

My father was radically saved while living as a hippie in Hawaii. He wanted to save the whales and get involved in Greenpeace there. However, living as a beach bum, he knew he was empty. He stumbled upon a Christian revival service after deliberating between that and a Buddhist temple across the street that was also having a meeting. He was the only one who showed up for the evangelistic gathering, and to the eternal credit of the pastor and his wife, they went through the order of service as though there were a packed house instead of one dirty hippie sitting in the last row with his feet in flip-flops propped up on the pew in front of him.

When the invitation time came, the pastor said, "If there is anyone here tonight who wants to come forward and give their life to Christ, get up now." My dad looked to his left and to his right. He was still the only one there. He was searching and empty, and he wanted answers. His pulse raced. He sensed Jesus calling him. He got up out of his seat, flip-flopped his way down the aisle, and gave his life to Jesus. Nothing would ever be the same.

No longer aimless and wandering, my dad had purpose. The

five years he spent in college studying broadcasting that he was so disillusioned with would be put to great use by God, both as a way to pay the bills and as a tool to further the reach of the gospel through Christian media. Working at companies like the TV station FOX provided him with consistent income while he pursued ministry in ways that didn't bring him a paycheck. He also put his media know-how to kingdom work by helping churches all over the country launch radio programs and radio stations. He served as an assistant pastor at a handful of ministries from California to Florida, and he planted two churches in the state of Colorado, where I grew up in and around TV stations, radio studios, and church plants.

Unlike when I was a kid, I now make my own fashion decisions, but I still want to be like my dad when I grow up. He was the best man in my wedding and is a great man of God who loves Jesus and cares for people. Thinking back to his move to Hawaii—which he thought would give him the chance to live free, save whales, and grow his beard and hair out—it's easy to see now that the real reason he went there was so he could meet Jesus. Had he zigged when he should have zagged, how different life would be—and not just for him. I wouldn't be here today had he, for instance, gone to the Caribbean instead.

My mom, Sky, had her own encounter with Jesus. She was raised in a home with money and power but little happiness. When she met my dad, they were both on a quest for ultimate meaning that took them from an abandoned adobe house in Taos, New Mexico, to the Bahamas, where they lived on coconuts and wild beans and rice. They parted ways: him to Hawaii and salvation, and her to Michigan, where a girl from Campus Crusade for Christ shared the gospel with her and she ended up becoming a Christian.

My dad wrote her a letter telling what had happened in his life, and they decided to get married and serve the Lord together.

BREAKING BAD

My story of coming to faith in Christ is in many ways the exact opposite of my parents'. They grew up without God and knew how empty the wells of this earth are, having looked everywhere to find something to fill them, but I grew up being told Jesus is the answer.

Food was not the only extremely healthy thing in our home. Psalty the Singing Songbook (a freakishly blue, inexplicably happy human-book hybrid), *Superbook*, *The Greatest Adventure: Stories from the Bible*, and *Colby the Computer* composed most of my entertainment choices as a child. *VeggieTales* hadn't been invented yet, and being a child of the 80s in a Christian bubble felt extremely restrictive. My friends watched *He-Man and the Masters of the Universe*, but I wasn't allowed to. My mom thought it was too violent, and there was someone named Skeletor, who was surely occultic, in it. (I find it ironic that now I travel the country to put on events called Skull Church, named after Skull Hill, the place where Jesus died.)

This sheltered upbringing lead to a revolt. Suppressing my inner sense of calling, I entered middle school and was exposed in short order to porn, bad language, and shoplifting. Just as I had binged on sugar and soft drinks when I could get my hands on them in elementary school, as a sixth grader I embraced this much more serious behavior as though I had discovered a secret treasure. Having been warned about sin since I was small, I wanted to see for myself what the world had to offer. The worst part was that I kept up the facade at church. I was living a double life, and I was growing miserable. As the adage goes, I had too much of the truth in me to be happy in the world, but too much of the world in me to be happy in the truth.

I am not sure how much of what I was up to—if any—my parents were aware of at the time, but when I was in eighth grade, they moved me to a Christian school. Things went from bad to worse. I quit shoplifting after someone close to me got busted and I was scared straight. But now in addition to watching porn and using bad language, I smoked cigarettes, drank alcohol when I had the chance, and tried pot on a few occasions. Being a skater was the cool thing, so I fashioned myself into one and tried to act and dress like the popular kids at school. I dutifully listened to Nirvana and even took sandpaper to my shoes to make them look as though they had been worn down through a thousand kickflips (which I couldn't actually pull off).

Those years are among the most difficult of my life. I was empty and got picked on relentlessly. I was smaller than most of the other kids in my grade, had buckteeth, and wore glasses. I tried a few sports but found them difficult because I have asthma, and I'm sure the smoking was not doing me any favors. What I lacked in physical ability I made up for with a quick tongue and a lot of sass, but this attitude didn't help with the bullying. I was given the nickname "Ratboy" and merely tolerated by the group of "friends" I wanted desperately to be accepted by. My inner loathing was fierce, which led to me lashing out at my family and anyone at school lower on the social totem pole than I was (a very, very short list). Thoughts of suicide were often not too far from my mind.

The lame thing about this situation is that it was all so unnecessary. I knew better. I had originally thought my parents were trying to keep me from fun, but I was discovering that after you get through the candy coating, all sin has to offer is heartbreak, bitterness, and regret.

In high school everything changed. I gave my heart to Jesus. Nothing so dramatic as my dad's conversion in Hawaii, but I, too, was at a beach: New Mexico's Elephant Butte Lake. Glamorous, huh? I was with the youth group from my church on a weekend trip, and God made my heart sing.

It was the people as much as the message that changed me. The leaders and volunteers made an indelible impact on me just by their love. They cared about me and were nice to me. I felt as though I belonged. All those feelings of insecurity, sadness, and turmoil I had been carrying around came to the surface, and I realized I was desperately lonely. All it took was people in their twenties, older and cooler than any of the kids at school whose opinions mattered so much to me, being kind to me. Something inside me began to break. I wanted to know and be known. In this group of Christ followers, I found community.

Throughout the weekend I began to wrestle with uneasiness. I felt a nagging suspicion deep down that God was calling my name. I heard it in my bunk before bed as clearly as I did during quiet moments when I looked at the water. I sensed his whisper during late-night conversations with one of the camp counselors while we made s'mores at the bonfire. Deep was calling unto deep.

It came to a head during a gospel invitation at one of the gatherings. The gospel was explained as I had heard it a thousand times: We are all sinners, separated from God by the wrong things we have done. Jesus died on the cross to pay for the sins of the world. He rose from the dead, defeating the power of death.

If you turn from your sin and turn to him in faith, you will be forgiven and will receive everlasting life.

As the speaker extended the invitation for people to come to Jesus, I felt the unmistakable need to get up out of my seat and respond. My heart was beating out of my chest, and my hands started to sweat. It suddenly became clear to me that God wasn't interested in getting just the hour out of my week when I attended church; he wanted every bit of my heart and my life—twenty-four hours a day, seven days a week. He wanted all of me.

I began to fidget, fighting the conviction. I wanted to respond. I needed to respond. I needed to cross this line and take a stand, giving my life to Jesus. But I was afraid: afraid of what others would think about me.

I have been going to church my whole life! My dad works at the church! If I indicate that I need to give my life to Jesus, everyone will think I am a fake and a hypocrite and a phony.

These thoughts, along with snapshots of the sinful life I'd been living, whipped through my mind like a sandstorm. *I am a hypocrite and a fake and a phony,* I realized. I fought through the tangled web of my need to please others and gave my heart and life—past, present, and future—to Jesus. I went all in.

Corrie Ten Boom's sister Betsie said, "There is no pit so deep that He is not deeper still."[1] That's how God rolls. He is better at saving than you could ever be at sinning. I didn't earn it and couldn't deserve it, but I had been set free. As Job once said, I had heard of God with the hearing of my ear, but now my eyes had seen him (Job 42:5).

Following Jesus is the best decision I have ever made. I was baptized on the beach under the watchful eye of a rock that looked a bit like an elephant. I went home a different person.

KILLER DANA

It wasn't long before I began to sense that God had plans that had been uniquely created for me. I began to understand that there was a call on my life, that I was destined for impact. Just as when I was a kid, I felt myself drawn to thoughts of becoming a pastor.

Charles Spurgeon, one of the most punk-rock preachers the world has ever seen, once advised a group of young men he was mentoring not to go into the ministry if they could help it. If you can do anything else, he told them, do it! Be a banker, practice law, be a surgeon, and glorify God by doing so. Only become a pastor, he advised, if you literally can't not. Do it only if, as it was with Jeremiah, God's Word is a consuming fire inside your bones and you are unable to hold it back.[2]

I see the wisdom of those words now, having experienced both the delights and the difficulties of being a pastor, but as a young man it was as though Darth Vader's tractor beam were sucking me into preaching, and resistance was futile. I just knew in my heart that one day I would plant and pastor a church, probably in a big city on the east coast.

After attending a Bible college in California, I moved back to Albuquerque, New Mexico, and apprenticed under Pastor Skip Heitzig, a wonderful man of God who taught me how to teach God's Word at his church, Calvary of Albuquerque. It was during this season that I met and married a gorgeous and godly girl named Jennie.

She had moved to the desert to take part in a yearlong missions internship at the church before returning to central California, where she had been raised. As I got to know her, I decided I wasn't going to let her out of my sight. Jennie is the nicest person I have ever met. She is compassionate, generous, and sweet. I can actually feel myself becoming a better human when I am around her, and I tell her all the time that if she ever leaves me, I'm coming with her.

We served for a few years in Albuquerque, where I was the youth pastor over the same student ministry that I had been saved in, before we were offered a position at a church in Orange County, California. We had just found out that we were pregnant with our first child, and it was an exhilarating adventure for Jennie and me to pack up and move to the beach, living away from both of our parents and forging our own family identity.

We soon fell into a rhythm we loved. We lived in Dana Point, a small town right on the Pacific Ocean, made famous for a surf break the Beach Boys used to sing about nicknamed "Killer Dana." Humpback whales pass the break on their annual trek from Alaska to Hawaii. I took up surfing, gained ten pounds from all the In-N-Out burgers I ate, and bought season passes to Disneyland. Our first daughter, Alivia Sky, was born in a hospital in Laguna Beach that had an ocean view. We had a scare when she came out with her umbilical cord wrapped around her neck. Her face was blue, and she wasn't breathing. But the doctors acted fast, and we brought her home healthy and happy. Life was good.

In addition to overseeing the student ministry, my responsibilities at the church regularly included preaching to the adults in the main worship center when the senior pastor was out of town. I was developing as a communicator and started to receive invitations to speak at events in other places. When the senior pastor resigned, the board of directors named me interim teaching pastor, and I was thrust into the main pulpit on a regular basis. It was terrifying and exciting to preach to thousands of adults as a twenty-two-year-old greenhorn, but the church took to me, and my prospects for the future looked good.

If it were up to me, I think I would have stayed in California forever. Surfing, preaching, and going to Disneyland—a guy could do worse. We could have had a happy life there. But God had other plans.

OUR GATORADE JUST FROZE

About this time I started to have this growing restlessness inside me. It was like a maternal clock that a woman who is pushing forty but has no husband or kids might hear ticking—only my clock was telling me that it was time to go BASE jumping for Jesus.

> MY CLOCK WAS TELLING ME THAT IT WAS TIME TO GO BASE JUMPING FOR JESUS.

At such a young age, I had chanced upon a ministry jackpot. My gig was cush. Don't get me wrong—there were challenges as there are in every church, but I had it pretty easy. A little too easy.

I started to think a lot about butterflies and how if you cut them out of their cocoons or help them out in any way, they will never develop the strength they need in their wings to be able to achieve takeoff. They have to struggle out in order to come into their own. Flight only comes after the fight. I felt as though I needed to go after my childhood dreams about church planting and launch out into the deep if I was to become all that God wanted me to be. Continuing on the current path made sense from a career trajectory perspective, but would it short-circuit my spiritual development and stunt my growth?

Around that time I had been asked to speak at an outreach event being organized in Montana. A California businessman named Bob Osborne, who grew up vacationing in Montana, desired to see people in Kalispell come to know Jesus, so he booked some bands, rented a rodeo arena, and brought me in to speak. After the event he told me I should move there and start a church. I assured him I would pray about it—but I didn't intend to at all.

Too honest? Sorry. It's true. I am Jacob, not Esau. Urban Outfitters, not REI. I'll take a cup of coffee and a solid Internet connection over a hike through the woods any day. Malls, yes—Montana, no. Plus, it didn't make any sense. I felt a call to bring the gospel to millions of people. Montana doesn't even have a million warm bodies in it, unless you count deer. (For the record, I don't count deer.) In addition, Jennie and I had been doing events to communicate a fresh perspective on life, death, sex, and romance, called The O2 Experience, that had been gaining traction, and I had this idea to start an evangelistic event called Skull Church that would be like a guerilla gospel crusade. Both of these events made sense in metropolitan areas, not in the sticks. I was also toying with the idea of planting a church in a new Orange County master-planned community called Ladera Ranch.

But I couldn't get the idea of moving to Montana out of my head. It was like a splinter in my soul. I would stay up at night thinking about it. And the more I did, the more convinced I became that I was supposed to go there and start a church. Paul had his man from Macedonia who showed up in a dream while he was trying to get to Asia and begged him to come to Europe, and I had a man speaking up for Montana on the phone. Bob Osborne had bought a bar, and he had fixed up a room above it that he was willing to lease me for a dollar for a year if I wanted to use it to start a church. No strings attached.

To make matters more confusing, at this same time I started to get job offers from several megachurches, including one from my all-time hero, the pastor and evangelist Greg Laurie. It was completely disorienting to have so many options on the table. I needed counsel. I needed a magic map to jump out of a backpack. I needed Yoda.

I made an appointment to see the wisest person I knew, Pastor Chuck Smith. He is the founder of the Calvary Chapel network of churches and practically a character out of the Bible. He has since gone to heaven, but when I met with him he was still preaching and healthy. I explained my conflict: I enjoyed preaching in California and appreciated the opportunities I had been given there, but I wanted an adventure, a venture in faith. I wanted to launch out into the deep and let my nets down. I told him of the Montana idea and the other options. After describing my confusion, I waited for him to tell me God's will for my life. He refused to do so. He simply told me, "Levi, people need Jesus everywhere. There is no wrong answer."

I don't know if I left more frustrated or relieved. But in time I saw the wisdom of his response. Had he told me what to do, I probably would have done it, or at the very least put a lot of stock in his opinion. By forcing me to make my own decision and hear God for myself, he was helping me to develop the muscles of my faith that I so desperately needed.

We decided to move to Montana. One of the things that finally helped me make up my mind was when another pastor friend told me that it was a no-brainer to stay in California. "If you move to a rural part of the country and things go very well," he said, "you might get to minister to a few hundred people after several painful years. Here in California," he continued, "you have the opportunity to minister to thousands of people." Something inside me stiffened. In the moment, I nodded my head at his logic, but later I reflected on the conversation in my journal and wrote, "What if God wants me to go to Montana *and* minister to thousands of people?"

Jennie and I decided we would give it five years and then reassess. Worst-case scenario, we could always go back to California if God didn't bless our efforts.

Once I announced that we were going, a number of people went out of their way to talk us out of it. Someone told me tongue in cheek, "You do know that you're planning on moving to a part of the country where it is so cold that cows die there in the winter—they just drop dead, frozen solid." *Cows die there.* His words rang in my head. What was I thinking?

One person I respected actually told me, "It is not God's will for you to go." That got my attention. Over pancakes he looked me in the eyes and said, "Levi, we need you here. There is a generation that is dying and going to hell by the truckload right here in the OC. Your ministry is effective here. You can't go." I couldn't argue with him, but all I knew was that I felt as though I would be disobedient not to move to Montana and preach the gospel.

It is hard to describe what it's like to leave sunny, always-seventy-five-degree Dana Point, California, and arrive in Montana in January, a month where it's always winter and never Christmas. It reached fourteen below zero within a few days of our arrival. It was so cold that when we were unpacking our moving truck, our Gatorades froze, in the bottles, between drinks.

What had I done?

FRESH LIFE

A few friends moved out with us to help start the church, and a few more planned to come within the next couple months. One packed up and left after being in the state for ten days; Montana just wasn't for him.

We put flyers up around town announcing the start of Fresh Life Church. On Sunday, January 14, we had our first service. Fourteen people showed up. The temperature outside was fourteen degrees Fahrenheit. Fresh Life was born.

Five years later, by my original date to reassess whether God was behind our move, we had seen three thousand people come to know Jesus through our weekend worship experiences and outreach events. The original church plant in Kalispell had grown to four campuses across the state—a number that is now six as of the publishing of this book, with a seventh in the pipeline. We owned and operated two full-power radio stations and now a half-dozen translator signals broadcasting live Fresh Life worship experiences plus music and Bible studies across the state. Our television show was on the CW channel in every major metropolitan area in Montana each Sunday morning. I was regularly being asked to travel around the country to speak to crowds numbering up to sixty-five thousand people. I thought I was walking away from so many possibilities by moving to the wilderness, but God blessed my willingness to embrace obscurity and lay down everything I had by giving me even more opportunities.

None of it was easy. There were plenty of challenges on the way. Growth brought complexity and difficulty. I had to go through pastoral puberty and find out who God called me to be. People left the church who I thought would stay. I snapped my femur in half in a snowmobile accident. Our second-born had serious allergies that took us a few years to get our heads around before we adjusted to the challenges of what she could eat. In the same year both my parents had nearly fatal cardiac events, one after the other, that put my brothers, sisters, and me on an exhausting emotional roller coaster.

Looking back it is easy to see all the dots that God connected to unfold his plan. Not so much in the moment. Life in real time is messy. The fingerprints of God are often invisible until you look at them in the rearview mirror. Just as God's calling became clearer over time for my dad, mom, Jennie, our daughters, and me, if you don't get impatient, his plans will become increasingly apparent to you.

THE FINGERPRINTS OF GOD ARE OFTEN INVISIBLE UNTIL YOU LOOK AT THEM IN THE REARVIEW MIRROR.

We treat the subject of God's will as though it were this crazy, exotic, mysterious thing, but in truth it's far less cryptic than that. Discerning God's calling is more a relationship than a route, more journey than destination. It's about who you are becoming more than where you are going. Perhaps it's less about *what* you do and more about *how well* you do whatever you do. It's not something you have to sit around waiting for; it's something that's all around you, even now. It's here and it's ready, if you would just open your eyes.

We get hung up on the particulars of God's concealed will, but—assuming you are walking with him and obeying his revealed will—you can do what you want or go where you want and trust that he is the one leading and guiding through your thoughts and desires. Psalm 37:4 says, "Delight yourself in the LORD, and he will give you the desires of your heart" (ESV).

I never heard God say, "Move to Montana." I was walking with him and went on a hunch. Because I was open to his leading and guiding—though it scared me at the time—I went with it and stepped out in faith. In retrospect, I can see that his fingerprints were all over it. He went before us and set things up, guided us in his providence, and prepared things for us to discover, just as he put that faithful preacher in my dad's path in Maui. But these are things you can't see until you look back. You just have to believe they will be there as you keep moving forward.

Our church wasn't the only thing to grow. Our firstborn daughter, Alivia, was followed by three more beautiful girls: Lenya, Daisy, and Clover. God truly did exceedingly and abundantly more than we could ever have imagined. We built a house and fell in love with Montana. I even began to appreciate outdoorsy stuff like camping—in small doses—though technically I think you would call it "glamping" since we make runs back to town for Vietnamese takeout and lattes. Our national events began to take off as well. We continued The O2 Experience and started Skull Church. Both have found great success, with thousands and thousands of lives touched by the gospel from coast to coast.

True to the promise of Jesus, as we sought first the kingdom of God and his righteousness all these things were being added to us (Matthew 6:33). We were living out things we wouldn't even have dared to dream.

THREE

THE CHRISTMAS FROM HELL

How could anyone plan a funeral for their five-year-old child? I shuddered and pushed the thought as far away from me as I could. I pulled my own five-year-old closer to my chest and planted a kiss on the top of her head. I was reading on my iPad about the memorial services for the victims of the Sandy Hook Elementary School shooting in Newtown, Connecticut. My daughter Lenya, always the early riser, was sitting on my lap, snuggling me as she did nearly every morning. We had nicknamed her "Lenya Lion" for her ferocious personality and full head of hair, which had been wild and mane-like since birth. She watched *Mickey Mouse Clubhouse* on the TV as I read the news and drank coffee.

Death doesn't always call ahead. It comes to us in a lot of ways, but often it is a surprise. "Sir, you have six months to live" is not something anyone wants to hear, but if your doctor says that to you, know that it is a gift. Not just for you—because it forces you to confront your mortality and gives you the chance to prepare—but for everyone who loves you as well, because they will get the chance to say good-bye. When the parents of the children from Newtown put them on the bus or dropped them off at school, they had no idea what was going to happen that day, and they will spend the rest of their lives wishing they could have seen it coming.

So, too, when death came to our home, it blindsided us. To say that we weren't expecting it is putting it mildly. It came out of nowhere and delivered a sucker punch so fast that we didn't have the chance to even think about flexing. Like a thunderous blow to the solar plexus, it knocked the wind out of us and left us gasping for breath on an emergency room floor. Soon after, stunned and completely in shock, we were getting into our car in the hospital parking lot, only there was one fewer seat belt buckled. Horrified, I looked in the rearview mirror at the gaping hole where my daughter should be sitting.

It was a Thursday. In our house, Friday is Family Day. It was all planned out. Breakfast out, ice skating, and a special dinner at a fancy restaurant. A dance party in the middle. Music and laughter. Giggles and snuggles. Lots of wardrobe changes. There are five women and one man in the Lusko entourage. I am a minority in a sorority. On any given day there might be fifteen or twenty different outfits. And that number would go way up if you include Jennie and the girls.

Anyway, our plan for Friday was that Lenya, my second oldest, and I were going to break off from the herd and go to Target so she could buy Christmas presents for her sisters and I could buy her a Barbie she had earned with hearts from her heart chart.

Family Days are always important. Sacred. A day of rest. Sabbath. Recharging batteries and replenishing relationships. Twitter, texting, Instagram, and e-mail are not welcome. We are

Amish for a day. The girls are allowed to call us out if we break these rules and do anything but dote on them and smell the flowers. I have more violations in my file than Jennie does. You don't know trouble if a three-year-old hasn't gotten in your face and scolded you for "texting on Famwy Day!"

This Friday, Family Day was extra meaningful. We needed it. The past week had been extremely intense. We were in the ramp-up for nine Christmas services at our church that would begin Saturday. There had been extra meetings and events filling up not only days but nights as well. The staff Christmas party was one night. A dinner with a group of students my wife and I had been investing in was another. There was the taping of a video special looking back at 2012 that we would play in our church campuses across the state in the lead-up to the new year. The week was packed, much worse than normal.

We had told the girls, "This is crazy, but Friday is coming!" It was going to be a much-needed calm between two storms. I had made a dinner reservation at a special restaurant we had never taken the girls to. We were going to get dressed up and have a ball.

It seems cruel to me now, thinking about what that Friday was going to be like. You can't get to Friday without going through Thursday, and on Thursday, December 20, the bottom dropped out.

When I am working on a message I'll be preaching, there is a fire under me as Saturday and Sunday approach. The process begins on Monday, and I prefer for it to end on Thursday so that I am able to enjoy Friday without it looming over me. I usually have to go into lockdown on Thursdays, working as if the devil were at my heels, until I get it done. Because this message was for Christmas—one of the two times of the year that our attendance swells dramatically, with friends and family members more likely to accept an invitation—there was even more self-imposed pressure.

At times writing a message feels like wrestling an octopus to the ground in the dark, but on this day it flowed, and I was happy to be making such great progress. I took a late afternoon lunch break to work out. When I got home, my family was about to leave to run errands and then attend a birthday party. Lenya bent down, carefully untied my red Nikes, and pulled them off my sweaty, stinky feet.

I got frustrated when I realized I was saying good-bye for the evening. I had just a little bit of work to do on my message, but because of a late-night scooter party illuminated by my headlights, my car battery was dead. With no car, I would be stuck at home and unable to join them when I finished. Oh well. I hugged them all and helped load them in the car.

Lenya forgot her jacket. I went back to get it and handed it through the window.

"Thanks, Dad. I love you," she said.

It was the last time I would hear her voice or see her smile.

NIGHTMARE BEFORE CHRISTMAS

When I finished my message the house felt so empty. I wished I were with the girls at the party. As the day gave way to night, Jennie arrived by herself. She had gone to the birthday party with Alivia, Lenya, Daisy, and Clover and then dropped the girls off at her mom's so she and I could wrap Christmas presents. To be completely honest, I didn't do any wrapping. We ate some pasta in front of the fire, and as she wrapped, I put *Home Alone* on and watched Macaulay Culkin's character, Kevin, outsmart the Wet Bandits. I actually made her job much more difficult, doing my best to distract her from wrapping by trying to get her to make out with me. (It's okay, we're married.)

She finished with the gifts, and we got in the car to pick the girls up, texting her mom that we were coming. On the five-minute drive I announced, "I just feel so relaxed right now." That stands out to me, because I am generally about as tightly wound as the inside of a baseball. Relaxing takes effort for me. But I meant what I said. Thinking of the Family Day ahead of us and how happy I was to spend some quality time with the girls after a busy week put me at ease.

We pulled up to the house, and immediately the tranquility broke. The door burst open and Jennie's younger brother ran out to meet us, yelling about Lenya not breathing. Jennie ran in to find her mom, Sylvia, trying to give Lenya an asthma treatment. Lenya looked up and saw her mommy enter the room just before her eyes rolled back and she lost consciousness.

Lenya had gotten a little wheezy while sitting on the couch playing an iPhone game. This is not unusual. I have had asthma almost all my life (I have an inhaler right here with me as I type), and both Lenya and her older sister, Alivia, have it too. We keep their medicine with them at all times. It always works. But this time it didn't put a dent in the attack. Her breathing just got worse. Jennie's mom had tried to call us, but Jennie's parents live in a cellular dead spot, so once we turned onto their road, we lost all service.

By the time I got into the kitchen, Lenya had already blacked out. I rushed to her and took over, putting the nebulizer into her mouth. Something formed in my stomach that clawed at me. Fear.

As if I were watching storm clouds gathering in the sky, I sensed myself beginning to panic. She wasn't breathing.

I told Sylvia to call 911, and I began to do CPR as well as I could remember while an ambulance was dispatched. Jennie was hysterical, and I wanted to join her. I remember her crying out to God and begging Lenya to breathe over and over again as I gave chest compressions with trembling hands. I put my lips to Lenya's and felt my breath fill up her lungs. God gave me the strength to remain calm, to be there, to fight for her. I felt her take one shallow breath and thought she was coming back to us, but it never happened again.

When the paramedics arrived and took over, I saw it in their faces. As they worked to save Lenya, I asked one question: "Is her heart beating?"

One of them answered, "No, not right now."

Everything in me sank. I could see she was hooked up to a defibrillator. When I asked why it wasn't shocking her, someone said, "It will if it can."

The paramedics loaded her into the ambulance, and we raced to the hospital. The same hospital where Lenya was born. My blood, hot with adrenaline, flashed through my veins. I felt helpless, dizzy, and frantic. I prayed. In the ER waiting room, Jennie and I held each other and begged God for a miracle—until the doctor appeared to tell us there was nothing they could do. Would we like to go in and be there as they stopped working?

We pushed past him and raced behind the curtain. We fell on our knees and pleaded for the God who made the sun stand still and raised Jesus from the dead to send Lenya back into her body. Instead, the sun set.

I had seen God do the impossible in my life. Dreams had come true. Now, my worst nightmare had too. I would have died on the spot if it could have helped her. But I wasn't given that option. There was no miracle. Her body remained motionless. She was pronounced dead.

This couldn't be real. I felt as though I were watching everything happen from outside myself.

When a woman's husband dies, she is called a widow. If it's the husband who survives, he becomes a widower. Children who lose their parents are called orphans. But what do you call a mom or a dad who has had to face the death of a child? There is no title for that. I suppose that is because there really are no words to describe such a thing.

We were shattered. Devastated. We didn't know what to do. The medical personnel cleared the room.

Waves of suffocating sorrow threatened to smother us. We sobbed from the depths of our souls. If tearing my heart from my chest would have helped Lenya, I would have done it. I hated the world for not having her in it any more. I always thought I would die young. Never did I think my child would.

Even so, our anchor held.

Though we were afraid, we were not alone. We experienced peace that passes understanding. Everything we preached in the sunshine we believed in this valley—the valley of the shadow of death. We lifted our hands to the air, right there in the ER, and blessed the name of the God who gives and takes away. Just as we dedicated Lenya to him when she was born, we committed her to him again. We thanked him for the honor of being her parents and for five beautiful years with her. We confessed our faith in the resurrection of Jesus and put our hope in him anew. On the floor of the emergency room, we intuitively sensed that our worship was

> EVERYTHING WE PREACHED IN THE SUNSHINE WE BELIEVED IN THIS VALLEY—THE VALLEY OF THE SHADOW OF DEATH.

linked to the pulse and frequency of heaven. We felt a nearness to her in it, and we leaned into it. We were on holy ground.

We held her hands. Even with the tubes and the equipment and the wires, she was stunningly beautiful. We kissed her face and stroked her hair and cried. Her eyes were open. She was wearing pajamas. Red leggings, a T-shirt, and socks. Her shirt had been cut open. I reached out and closed my little Lenya Lion's eyes.

The doctor later explained that medically she was coded as nonresponsive by the time the paramedics arrived. Simply put, she was already in heaven before we got to the hospital. Strangely, that brought me comfort, knowing that Lenya's final moments on earth were with us and not strangers. Her mother's voice was in her ears, and she was held by her daddy's hands as I gave her CPR. She went straight from my arms to the arms of her Heavenly Father in paradise. Lenya had gone home for Christmas.

We, on the other hand, were stuck here on this fallen planet, about to experience the furthest thing from a heavenly Christmas as you could get. Within the space of a half hour, the nurse was asking us which funeral home we wanted to use. It made me angrier than I can tell you to think about a phone ringing and someone coming to zip up her body in a bag and cart it off to a funeral home. I felt myself shaking and my teeth clenching together.

By this point Lenya's three sisters were in the hospital waiting room. Alivia, seven at the time, was the only one awake. She asked where Lenya was. We told her that Lenya was with Jesus in heaven.

These girls were not just sisters. They were best friends, classmates, partners in crime. Peas and carrots, those two.

Alivia processed this news, and then she began to cry. "Stacia told me she was going to be okay," she sobbed. Stacia is her aunt who was eleven at the time. When the ambulance had come, they had watched Lenya being loaded up, and Stacia had tried to comfort her niece by telling her she was going to be okay. We assured Alivia that Stacia was right and that Lenya was better than okay—she was perfect.

SHOCK AND AWE

Leaving the hospital without Lenya that night was nearly intolerable. It went against every instinct in my body. We had brought her home from this very building only five years ago. Taking care of her safety was my job. I put her helmet on her when she so much as looked at her bike, spent hours obsessing over the perfect installation of her car seat (with and without LATCH clips), and kissed every single owie. Now we were supposed to just leave and go home?

It was now Friday, December 21. Thursday had come and gone. There would be no Fun Friday Family Day. No sleeping in or breakfast out. There would be no music or dancing. Our flag was at half-mast. Lenya and I would not go together to Target to buy her a Barbie doll. The money she had saved to buy gifts for her sisters would not be spent. The hour of our reservation at the fancy restaurant would come and go without us. "Lusko, table for six" would not be called. For the first time since Clover's birth, we were now five. By cruel coincidence this day was the winter solstice, the first day of winter and the longest night of the year. In every sense of the word it would be the longest day ever.

Nobody asks to be in an emergency. We certainly didn't. Death doesn't call ahead.

As we sat there in the car in the parking lot of the hospital, attempting to bring ourselves to perform the impossible task of physically leaving our Lenya Lion behind, Jennie turned to me and said, "You need to go back in there and invite those people to church."

I must not have heard her right. Leaving was torture, and she wanted me to go back in and have to leave *again*?

I looked at her. "What?!"

She repeated herself: "You should invite them to Christmas at Fresh Life." The message I had written Thursday was in preparation for the nine times I was supposed to preach in just a few short days. It seemed like a hundred years ago that I had been working on that sermon, but all of a sudden I tumbled back to reality. Jennie handed me some invitations to our Christmas Eve services. Where she produced them from I will never know, but because of the serious, determined look on her face, I took them from her.

I should pause here and tell you that my wife is the most amazing person I have ever met, especially when it comes to remembering to invite people to come to church. Once when we were getting ready to go to the hospital so she could have a baby, she went back into the house to get something. I realized a moment too late I should get it for her and went inside, only to find her leaning against a wall having a contraction but clutching some invitations to an event we were having the next week. When the contraction finished she said, "I'll need these to invite people in the birthing ward to Skull Church."

After handing me the Fresh Life Christmas invitations, Jennie told me, "It's what Lenya would want you to do." I knew she was right. Lenya followed in the footsteps of her momma in so many ways and would regularly encourage us to invite to church the gal who checked us out at the grocery store or a mom at the park. In fact, the next day we opened up one of the many purses Lenya owned, the one that she'd most recently been carrying around with her, and found her little Bible inside, along with some of the same invitations for Fresh Life Christmas.

I took the cards and walked back into the emergency room. With tears streaking down my face, I approached the nurses' station and began handing them out. I pointed to the room where I had just left and said, "My little girl, whose body is right there behind that curtain, is in heaven with Jesus because she trusted in him. And in three days we're going to celebrate Jesus' birth into our world. In her honor, I would like to invite all of you to come. I'm supposed to be the one to speak, and I'm not quite sure how yet, but if you will come, I will preach."

When we got home, all five of us collapsed in the queen-size bed Jennie and I share. There wasn't room for all of us, but we needed to be together, and sleep eluded us anyway. Waking up every twenty minutes or so and remembering what had just happened was horrific. For the next several months, nighttime and first thing in the morning remained the most difficult to get through. Something about darkness makes everything scarier and exaggerated.

After finally falling asleep for a full hour, I opened my eyes only to have what happened hit me with the impact of a sickening car accident once more. I looked beside me, saw all of my children except one, and felt hot tears spill down my face. For the first time in my life, I cried so much that my contacts fogged and I couldn't see. It would be a couple of days before I was able to wear them instead of my glasses, and it would be thirty-two days before I would make it through a day without weeping. I remember because after a month of almost nonstop tears, on that day, they didn't come. Instead I felt numb.

C. S. Lewis wrote, "Crying is all right in its way while it lasts. But you have to stop sooner or later, and then you still have to decide what to do."[1] When your heart is broken, you don't know where to go. Colors lose their brightness, and the world seems so gray. The ground is unsteady, and food tastes like ash. Your stomach flutters in a free fall that doesn't stop. Your fists ball up, but there's nothing to fight. A screaming, heaving, sinking panic rises in your chest. It can't be outrun, won't be shut down, and refuses to be put out.

Fortunately, we didn't have to go through any of this by ourselves. From the moment they heard, though it was the middle of the night, our worship pastor and executive pastor and their wives were there for us. They have been with us since before the beginning of Fresh Life. More than friends, we are thick as thieves. They were there for us on our worst day and have been there each day since. There are very few things more defining than the people you choose to do life with. We will love them all with our whole hearts, to the grave. They were there to care, to cry, and to listen. I don't remember them saying anything except continual expressions of their love of Lenya. They didn't offer platitudes or verses or tell us it was going to be okay. They simply offered their presence. And it meant the world to us.

Soon there were new difficulties to face. While the world was shopping for last-minute Christmas presents, we had to pick out a casket, choose the clothes to bury Lenya in, and decide on a plot of ground in a cemetery. Impossible decisions. These are things a child is supposed to do for her parents, not the other way around, especially when she is in kindergarten.

To make things even worse, the funeral industry, in my opinion, is nasty. The people at the funeral home were very kind; I'm talking about the style. To have to deal with death is already bad, but the sense of graphic design is appalling. Nothing is clean, nothing is streamlined, and everything is awful. If you want chubby, naked baby angels, kitschy Precious Moments, and gaudy, awful everything, you are in luck. If your design aesthetic is more Apple than it is Hallmark, you will hate your choices. I wanted to throw up just looking through the casket catalogue, and not just because of what I was going through but because there were no options that weren't hideous. To make matters worse, we were under a time crunch. Christmas Eve was the next day, making options even more limited. We ended up picking a solid white casket with no embellishment and had the nasty batting and pillow it came with thrown away. We had a talented artist who loved Lenya customize the outside of it with a superspecial nautical design.

It took some time, too, to figure out where we would bury her. The cemetery we initially chose (and that I have ridden my bike by for years) rejected us. They told us it was only for members of their church. Awesome. The next one on our list told us they were completely full. No room at the inn. This was not going well. Finally, we found a vacancy, but we had to pick the plot immediately because the ground had to thaw for several days before the hole could be dug. What a harsh place we call home. Gatorade isn't the only thing that freezes in Montana.

With all these awful preparations looming over us, it was very difficult for us to put on Christmas music and open stockings on December 25. But for Alivia and Daisy and Clover's sake, we had to find a way. Their sister had died, but they had not, and they needed us to show that we still loved and cared about them. I can't imagine how much harder it would have been without them to keep us moving forward.

The girls' big Christmas present was a visit to Disneyland. We were supposed to fly to California the day after Christmas. We ended up burying Lenya's body that day instead. Our airplane took off without us as we stood shedding tears in a cemetery. Snowflakes melted as they hit our cheeks, the cold tore at exposed skin, and our breath became visible in front of us each time we exhaled, as we stared with horror and disbelief at the small, white box about to be lowered into the earth. Scripture verses and worship songs broke the silence as we stood there in shock, clinging to the promise of the resurrection like a drowning man holds on to a plank of wood in a shipwreck.

> WE STOOD THERE IN SHOCK, CLINGING TO THE PROMISE OF THE RESURRECTION LIKE A DROWNING MAN HOLDS ON TO A PLANK OF WOOD IN A SHIPWRECK.

It was difficult and traumatizing to confront death in such a savage and vicious way on a day that was supposed to be so much fun. If we did not have hope, I honestly don't know how we could have stood up to it. It was terrible to face it even with the promise that Christ has conquered the grave.

THE GIFT OF SIGHT

The night Lenya went to heaven, we received a call from the emergency room within a half hour of getting home. When I answered the phone and heard it was someone from the hospital, my heart leapt. Maybe there had been a mix-up, and Lenya had just sat up. It was the opposite. The hospital was calling to ask whether we would be willing to donate Lenya's corneas and heart valves.

I wish I could say my reaction was noble, sacrificial, and generous. It wasn't. Everything in me coiled and stiffened, and I felt myself bristle. To think of doctors cutting into my daughter made me want to break something. As Jennie and I talked and prayed about it, we thought about how Jesus was the first and ultimate organ donor. He donated his blood for us on the cross, and his righteousness was transplanted into our hearts.

Though we knew there was no wrong choice, we felt like this was what God wanted us to do. To think of a part of our daughter helping people see or enabling someone to go through lifesaving surgery that could give him or her more time to come to know Jesus was too beautiful of an opportunity to pass on.

Lenya was* extremely tender and compassionate. She had great instincts when it came to the well-being of those around her. She was constantly doing what she could to help cheer people up, which she usually accomplished by making them laugh. She was the official Lusko family court jester. Though it was and is painful to think about, we made the decision to give this precious and costly gift.

We were later notified that the transplants were successful. There are two people on this earth to whom my daughter gave the gift of sight. They literally see life through Lenya Lion's eyes.

I have also been given the gift of sight. Having my daughter

* Throughout this book I will refer to Lenya in the past tense. This is not only difficult to do, but it feels dishonest, as I know that she is today more alive than she has ever been. I do so for clarity and because she has finished her race and fought the good fight, not because her life is over.

travel to the distant shores of heaven has opened my eyes to things unseen. I will walk with a limp, but I am better for it. I, too, look at life through different eyes. But it's not just a gift for me—it's a gift I desperately want to share with you.

FOUR

TURN OFF THE DARK

That Christmas message I was writing during Lenya's last day on earth? It all started with Spider-Man. I love superhero movies in general. *Batman, Wolverine, Unbreakable*—I'm not picky. If it has a big budget and I don't have to do a lot of thinking, I can usually go along for the ride.

A few weeks before Lenya went to heaven, Jennie and I were in New York with a group of friends, one of whom was having a birthday. To celebrate I bought tickets to the new production of *Spider-Man* on Broadway. Bono and the Edge had worked on the soundtrack, and some pretty elaborate technical innovations had gone into Spider-Man's ability to fly over the audience by using the same gear that moves cameras over the action at the Super Bowl. The show had been pretty badly panned by critics when it opened, and a few cast members had been injured when equipment malfunctioned. It's no good when Spidey's web fails and he falls several stories, resulting in broken bones that leave him lying on the ground, moaning and groaning in front of a packed audience. But the show had been retooled, and the kinks were supposedly worked out by the time we went.

The experience was all right. Not terrible, but not great. Our seats ended up being bad, and even with the Green Goblin being chased around by a human spider wearing spandex, there was still a bit too much singing for my liking. But as we were walking out of the theater, lightning struck.

For some reason I was thinking about the Christmas sermon I would need to begin working on in the next couple weeks. When I looked back at the marquee over my shoulder and saw the big, bold letters—*Spider-Man: Turn Off the Dark*—I stopped.

The words tumbled around in my mind over and over. *Turn Off the Dark. Turn Off the Dark. Turn Off the Dark.*

It's an unusual phrase. You would usually say, "Turn on the light." You generally don't think about darkness being deactivated.

Just then we turned the corner and were smack dab in the middle of Times Square. In addition to being one of the most overwhelming places in the world, Times Square is at midnight still as bright as high noon. It is like ADD paradise. As far as the eye can see, skyscrapers covered in the highest-definition screens money can buy display an endless loop of advertisements, bathing everything in an unnatural electronic glow. Store logos pulsate; a naked cowboy (if you don't know what I'm talking about, don't worry about it—just promise me you won't Google it) and knockoff cartoon characters pose for pictures with tourists from Ohio; and an endless stream of people covers every square inch of Manhattan sidewalk like ants attacking a puddle of ice cream.

As we took in the surreal scene and noticed the impact of all the light on a dark city street, something clicked in my mind.

"Eureka!" I announced to no one in particular. "There's my Christmas message! Turn off the dark."

Inspiration usually hits at the oddest times, and I was having a full-on Archimedes-in-the-bathtub moment: Christmas is all about Jesus turning off the dark.

By the time we had gone a few blocks, I had my message loosely mapped out and was pretty lit up about it (pun intended). Back at the hotel I jotted down my notes and put the idea on ice until the week of Christmas.

THE MESSAGE

On Thursday, December 20, I pulled out my notes and spent the day locking the message in. My plan was to show that the light of Jesus' birth turned off the darkness of four things: loneliness, fear, despair, and guilt.

Loneliness

Every gift sends a message. God sent us himself, because he knew how desperately we needed him. We are like a Jet Ski with the kill switch pulled. No matter how many friends we have, separated from him there is something missing. That is how it's possible to feel lonely in the middle of a crowded room. There is no greater present than his presence. That's why Jesus' name was to be Immanuel, which means "God with us."

Fear

Jesus is the wonderful counselor who was sent to us to give us wisdom and free us from what frightens us. We live in very uncertain times. The economy seems fragile, and natural disasters lurk around every corner. They don't all make the news, but there is a mass murder in America every two weeks.[1] Like the light that causes cockroaches to scatter, the presence of Jesus' perfect love in the human heart drives out all fear.

Despair

Hopelessness reigns. Suicide now kills more people than car accidents do.[2] So many despair of life itself—not just down-and-outers, but up-and-inners too. Professional athletes, singers, actors, CEOs. People take their lives without realizing it's a permanent solution to a temporary problem. A generation wears long sleeves to hide the fact that they cut themselves. If you are reading this and are a cutter or struggle with thoughts of taking your life, please know this: I understand that the pain is real. But you don't need to hurt yourself or make yourself bleed; Jesus shed his blood for you. He died so you could live!

Guilt

Forgiveness is our biggest need, because sin is our biggest problem. All of us have crossed lines we know we shouldn't have. Heaven is like a roller coaster: you must be this tall to ride, but none of us measure up. Jesus came to pay our bills. If we trust Jesus, his righteousness gets deposited into our accounts, because on the cross our sin was placed on his shoulders.

The Christmas sermon was nearly written. Because of my light-bulb moment in New York, Thursday's prep time wasn't grueling, and the verses and illustrations fell into place. I was happy enough with it to be able to look forward to our planned Family Day without it hanging over my head. I put together an e-mail with the points and verses so that the creative department could prepare the graphics that would appear on the screens. As a breath of relief passed my lips, I clicked Send. I had no idea that in a little more than five hours, our lives would change radically.

I also didn't realize at the time that the sermon was incomplete. It was missing a crucial point. Yes, Jesus turned off the darkness of loneliness, guilt, despair, and fear, but there was another thing he extinguished. By the end of the evening the final bullet point would rudely intrude into our home: death.

There would be no getting away from it.

I'll never be able to escape the awfulness of those early days. Waking up and running to her empty room, panicking and delirious with grief. Falling to the floor, shaking and feeling my bones ache. Collapsing on her bed and holding her clothes to my chest.

Death. Our great enemy. The last enemy. It didn't schedule an appointment or knock before entering. Death crashed our party.

PREACH THE WORD, DAD!

Two days before Christmas, in Lenya's honor and because I didn't know what else to do, I kept the promise I made to the hospital employees and prepared to preach at the first of our nine worship experiences. My family and I spent the day in a daze, still very much in shock, making arrangements for the burial and celebration that were scheduled for the day after Christmas. When I pulled out my notes a few hours before the service and read what I had written, I immediately sensed what was missing, and I knew exactly how to fix it.

I pulled our family Christmas card off the fireplace mantel and opened it up, looking in disbelief at the beautiful pictures from the last time we posed for a photographer as a family of six.

The photos were taken in Bozeman, Montana, just a month and a half earlier. We were in town for a two-night Skull Church event. This particular excursion to Bozeman had not gone as planned. An unexpected storm dubbed "Brutus" had rocked southern Montana, turning freeways into ice rinks and bringing an unexpected foot of snow. Generally early November weather is still pretty mild, so we hadn't even brought proper winter coats on the trip, and we paid for it.

Brutus or not, we soldiered on. We have a pregame ritual where, before I go on stage, the girls give me a fist bump and tell me, "Preach the word, Dad!" People came to know Jesus at the events, and we had fun getting to know the town. I had told the girls that John Mayer lived in Bozeman, showed them a picture of him, and told them to keep an eye out as we explored the city. Happy memories.

As I held the glossy card and looked at the photos, I realized there would be a hole in every picture we took from here on out. Death had ripped Lenya from our lives, torn her from our hands. I thought of future events and the fact that she wouldn't be there waiting for me when I came offstage. I started to feel dizzy.

When I got to the last panel of the card I found what I was looking for, what I desperately needed at that moment. Right above a shot of the six of us standing on a snowy sidewalk with our backs up against a textured black wall was the text we had chosen, taken from 2 Timothy 1:10:

JESUS HAS ABOLISHED DEATH AND BROUGHT LIFE AND IMMORTALITY TO LIGHT THROUGH THE GOSPEL.

I flashed back to when we had chosen this particular verse. Every year Jennie and I go through the Bible together (something I highly recommend for married couples), using a reading plan from the YouVersion app we have on our iPhones. Though we don't actually sit down and read together, we both go through the same plan so we're reading the same verses each day. Then we can talk about what stands out to us. It's a rhythm we've found that works for us.

I had been plugging my way through 2 Timothy 1 with a cup of coffee in my hands. Halloween hadn't passed yet, so Christmas was nowhere on the radar, but when I read this verse it struck me as powerful. *Jesus has abolished death. Wow. That's killer,* I thought.

Boo-ya! The synapses that fired next somehow caused my thoughts to travel to Christmas, and I e-mailed the verse to my assistant with a note about it going on the Christmas card we send out to our church body and ministry partners across the country.

Thinking back on it, I'm still mystified. It's a great verse, but it doesn't exactly taste like eggnog. If it had been "Joy to the world" or "Behold the virgin shall give birth," I would understand, but honestly—when was the last time you sent out a Christmas card with the word *death* on it? 2 Timothy 1:10 has Easter written all over it, but the vibe doesn't scream, "Happy birthday, Jesus!"

Strangely enough, when I told Jennie about it later on she said, "When I read that chapter today and saw that verse, I thought the same thing!" Birds of a feather, I guess.

There was a problem at the printer; struggles in the creative process abounded. The original shipment came with an error, and the job had to be rerun. The cards that would have been sent out two weeks before Christmas, with plenty of time to be enjoyed in the holiday ramp-up, went out late. They wouldn't hit homes until four days before Christmas. As a result, many of our friends and supporters around the country, who were hearing the heartbreaking news of Lenya's sudden and unexpected departure to heaven through texts, tweets, and Instagram posts that began to spread virally, would open their mailboxes that afternoon only to find happy, smiling photos of our family with the proclamation that "Jesus has abolished death and brought life and immortality to light through the gospel."

All of a sudden the verse didn't seem like such an odd choice. It was perfect for this Christmas. Prophetic, even. Fitting for a holiday where our hearts were at half-mast.

SORROW UPON SORROW

The truth is, death is what Christmas is all about. Jesus came to turn off the darkness of death by turning on the Light. Hebrews 2:15 says Jesus came to release those "who through fear of death were all their lifetime subject to bondage." Christmas exists so there could be an Easter, so we could live with hope and die without fear.

We so badly need this message, because this screwed-up world is full of sorrow. Sorrow *upon* sorrow, actually. That was how Paul the Apostle described grief and loss. His friend Epaphroditus contracted a fatal disease while trying to get money to him in prison. Paul told the Philippians, "For indeed he was sick almost unto death; but God had mercy on him, and not only on him but on me also, lest I should have sorrow upon sorrow" (Philippians 2:27).

There you have it, straight from Paul's mouth, a three-word

description of what it's like to have someone you love die: "sorrow upon sorrow." The phrase is intense in the original Greek; it is a nautical term that describes waves crashing on the shore.[3] If you have experienced the magnitude of the grieving process, you know how appropriate the metaphor is.

Waves aren't clean and neat, especially when there is a swell or storm. They come in sets, but there is a randomness to the pattern that makes the ocean dangerous and unpredictable. And no matter how much of a rhythm you find in the walls of water that come surging toward the sand, you can never discount the possibility of a rogue wave coming out of nowhere. That's why the number one rule of the beach is "Never turn your back on the ocean." ("Don't feed the seagulls" is a close second, and my vote for number three would be "Never wear a Speedo.")

No wonder Paul compared grief to the viciousness of dangerous surf. Grief is powerful and unpredictable. Your skin flushes, your heart burns, and your eyes sting. It's very difficult to keep your thoughts collected, and all but impossible to keep your emotions at bay. With the exception of when you're under the influence of drugs or alcohol, grief is probably the most powerful mood/mind/body-altering state you can be in, especially in the initial shocking aftermath of the traumatic event that caused it.

There are supposedly stages of grief: denial and isolation, anger, bargaining, depression, and finally acceptance.[4] My experience is that these don't come so tidily as moving from one zone to another. It's messy and muddled. You move in and out of the stages at random. They swirl together like an ugly emotional cocktail. Like a novice surfer getting stuck in the foaming white water, when you manage to get up for a breath, out of nowhere comes a wave you didn't see that takes you over the falls and into

LIKE A NOVICE SURFER GETTING STUCK IN THE FOAMING WHITE WATER, WHEN YOU MANAGE TO GET UP FOR A BREATH, OUT OF NOWHERE COMES A WAVE YOU DIDN'T SEE THAT TAKES YOU OVER THE FALLS AND INTO A WASHING MACHINE OF PAIN.

a washing machine of pain. Then one day you feel good—and you feel bad for feeling good.

Sorrow upon sorrow upon sorrow, with a side of sorrow. This is what Paul was saying would be what was waiting for him if Epaphroditus had died. A prolonged emotional battle that wouldn't be easy or over quickly.

Hold the phones, you might be thinking. *Didn't Paul know he would see Epaphroditus again? Didn't Paul know that if Epaphroditus had died, he would have gone to a better place? Paul's tears would be completely unwarranted, because at that moment his friend would be walking through streets of gold onto a sea of glass and perhaps riding his own personal unicorn. Didn't Paul know that heaven is for real? Or hadn't he read the* New York Times *bestselling book that is now a major motion picture starring Greg Kinnear?*

For the record Paul *did* know that heaven is for real. He knew better than anyone.

How? He got to go there one time (2 Corinthians 12:2–4). #HumbleBrag

Many Bible teachers think it was when he was stoned (with rocks, not weed) in the city of Lystra in Acts 14. He died and eventually returned to earth, where he got up, dusted himself off, and went straight back to preaching.[5] What he saw while he was in heaven so affected him that he later told the Philippians to quit praying for him to get off death row because he wanted to go back. He said that to leave earth and go to heaven would be far better; living was Christ and dying would be gain (Philippians 1:21).

And yet he also clearly said that if Epaphroditus had died, he would have felt "sorrow upon sorrow," a turbulent emotional experience that would crash into his heart like a tsunami.

HURTING WITH HOPE

Here's something you need to know: *hurting with hope still hurts.* The sting of death might have been removed, but it still stings. It hurts like hell even when you know your loved one is in heaven. No, we might not sorrow as those who have no hope, but that doesn't mean we won't be sad.

We do a disservice anytime we try to rush people through the process of grief, as though it were spiritual to put a happy face on a horrible thing. Masking pain doesn't heal it any faster; it actually slows it down and stunts your rehabilitation. Expecting someone to bounce back as some sort of benchmark of holiness is kind of like asking a person who has had an arm amputated if he is over it yet. Believe it or not, my family and I were asked this question, but just like the person with no arm, we will never get over it. Yes, an amputee will have two arms in heaven, just as we'll have Lenya with us again in heaven. And here on earth that amputee will eventually learn to walk triumphantly with his loss, just as we will. But there will be something missing for the rest of our lives.

I trust my daughter is in heaven—as many are quick to remind me when they write encouraging notes—but that doesn't mean living without her is easy. I'm not going to sit here at my computer and tell you it was no big deal to have to face Christmas with our three daughters here on earth while Lenya's body was two miles away, lying in the funeral home that I still can't drive by without shaking and wanting to light myself on fire.

It's been so very hard. *Sorrow upon sorrow.* As I write these words, in a cabin at a lake, it has been 592 days since Lenya went home, and yet there are fresh tears spilling down my face. God has made me stronger, so the pain is not always unbearable, but the weight hasn't gotten any lighter.

I have hope, but I'm not happy about it.

What I have discovered, though, is that neither is God. He's not happy about it. He's furious. Not about hope, but that we would need it. That we would have occasion for it. That's why he warned Adam and Eve in the garden to at all costs avoid the forbidden fruit (Genesis 2:17). He knew that sin would trigger death. He never intended for us to struggle in the surf, with wave after wave of sadness crashing down upon us.

You see how Jesus really feels about grief and death in John 11. When confronted with the awfulness of the death of his friend Lazarus, and with sorrow upon sorrow playing in surround sound by Lazarus' sisters, Mary and Martha, he reacted viscerally. Jesus wept. He didn't hide his emotion or try to disguise his sadness. He didn't put sunglasses on or clumsily say, "It's okay! Lazarus has gone to a better place, everybody. He's probably playing football in my Father's house." No, he cried.

Even more shocking is what came next.

The Bible says twice that Jesus groaned in his spirit. This was no ordinary sigh. The Greek word used here means "to bellow with rage."[6] It is a word that is so strong it is normally used to describe the angry snorting of an agitated horse. Have you ever seen a horse that is ticked off? Ears back, one hind leg up on tiptoe, ready to kick the teeth out of the first person stupid enough to walk through the impact zone. And there's the telltale throaty, slow whinny escaping its teeth. You wanna give a wide berth to an animal like that.

So much for gentle Jesus, meek and mild. He was fuming. Absolutely outraged. Mad at death. Angry at the grave, at sin, at the devil. But he wasn't just angry—he was angry enough to do something about it.

I'm not talking about what he did in the moment, though that is impressive to be sure. He raised Lazarus from the dead, but that wasn't his endgame. Remember, Lazarus would have to die all over again. Any physical miracle is just a delaying of the inevitable. Jesus was always focused on the spiritual work, because that would last forever. He actually viewed it as a failure if people didn't believe, because then he would be able only to heal the sick and perform other physical miracles but not do the deeper things he had his sights set on. Isn't that remarkable? The thing we normally focus on—tangible demonstrations of God moving—was a failure to Jesus if it didn't accompany something greater that happened on an invisible level!

So what did Jesus do after raising Lazarus from the dead? He went on to defeat death in the most unlikely way ever—by dying.

There's a crazy detail to the classic underdog story of David and Goliath that often doesn't make the cut (pun) in Sunday school. David's slingshot was used only to bring Goliath down. He dealt the deathblow by chopping Goliath's head off with a sword he pulled from the giant's sheath. How punk rock is that? Similarly, Jesus used death, Satan's most powerful weapon, against him: "that *through death* He might destroy him who had the power of death, that is, the devil" (Hebrews 2:14, emphasis added).

But the power wasn't in dying. Anyone can do that. Wait long enough, and it will happen to you. Jesus didn't just die—he rose from the dead. His soul reentered his decaying body, and he got up! Unbelievably, he offers this same casket-exploding power to anyone who believes.

This is the gospel: Jesus turned off the dark.

Death has been stripped of its power: "Having disarmed principalities and powers, He made a public spectacle of them, triumphing over them in it" (Colossians 2:15). He took the bullets out of the devil's gun. Satan can still pull the trigger, but there are only blanks in the chamber. Instead of being terrified, we can actually look at death victoriously. This is what Paul meant when he said Jesus has abolished death.

But, you ask, *why do we still have to die?* For something that's been abolished, it seems as though business is booming. True, but remember this: God's not finished yet. If there is one thing you need to know about God, it's that he always gets the last word.

IF THERE IS ONE THING YOU NEED TO KNOW ABOUT GOD, IT'S THAT HE ALWAYS GETS THE LAST WORD.

The cool thing about the way the Greek word for *abolished* is used in 2 Timothy 1:10 is it appears in a unique form that is used to describe a future event in the past tense—something that hasn't happened yet, but because it is so certain to occur it can be referred to as having been completed already.

God is the only one who can use such language. We can't talk that way. There are any number of things that can stop us from doing what we set out to do. The weather could change, the flight could get canceled, there could be a wreck on the freeway.

That's why we have to build a buffer into all the promises we make to our kids. Should something pop up that keeps you from doing something you gave them your word on, World War III *will* in fact occur, regardless of the fact that the situation was out of your hands. This is why experienced parents talk to their children like attorneys:

> "We will make every attempt to visit an establishment that serves ice cream in the vicinity that surrounds our house within the time period including, but not limited to, this lifetime."

> "It is our strong desire to purchase shoes that are new to you before the year comes to a conclusion."

You have to carefully craft communication with your kiddos, remembering the little litigators they are, because the last thing you want is to end up in court with your four-year-old because you didn't take them to Pinkberry. "But Dad, you promised!" "No, I said we would try!" Never leave a loophole, and be warned: they smell fear.

God doesn't have to build any buffers in the promises he makes, because (a) he is outside time, and what he will do is already complete to him (insert sound effect of mind being blown); and (b) there is no one who can stop him, and nothing that can stand in his way.

The final destruction of death is still in the future. It hasn't happened yet, but it will. Not only will I see Lenya again, but I will hold the same body I held here, only better, because what the thief has stolen will be restored sevenfold (Proverbs 6:31)!

This is why it's crucial for you to see that we don't need to put a nice face on our pain or hurry people through a process that can't be rushed: the fact that our sadness doesn't go away makes our triumph even more powerful. Our faith works in the fire, and not just when life is fun. We can be hard-pressed and yet not crushed, struck down and yet not destroyed—not because we know general facts about the resurrection or that there is a heaven, but because we trust in the one who said that he is the resurrection and the life, who took the keys from death and hell, was dead, and lives forever. His name is Jesus, and he always leads us in triumph!

CARVED IN STONE

When Lenya went to heaven, we were faced with a thousand impossible decisions. One was to decide what we wanted her tombstone to say.

We were horrified. This was our harsh reality in the final days of "the most wonderful time of the year"—cemetery locations, casket finishes, and the words we wanted chiseled into granite above the tomb of our wild and spunky kindergartener. There were boxed and wrapped presents with her name on them under the tree, yet we had to pick out a box to bury her body in. I felt sadness sinking in at the thought of seeing her name in such a setting. From deep within my heart I felt hatred toward death and sensed a Holy Ghost defiance rising in my soul. The grave might not have gotten the memo yet, but it has already been destroyed.

The inscription we chose reads

LENYA AVERY LUSKO

followed by her birth date:

9–8–7

and the date that is the worst day of our lives but the best day of hers:

12–20–12

In between is a giant anchor with a banner containing those same words from Scripture that Jennie and I had read on our iPhones a few months prior, all without a clue as to what their ultimate significance would be:

JESUS HAS ABOLISHED DEATH AND BROUGHT LIFE AND IMMORTALITY TO LIGHT THROUGH THE GOSPEL.

PREACHING IN PAIN

It was Christmas Eve—time to make good on my commitment to share the message God had given me after watching Spidey in the Big Apple.

It was incredibly emotional and overwhelming to speak. I was a train wreck until moments before, alternately breaking down and feeling strong even while driving to the beautiful performing arts center our Whitefish campus had rented for the first of our services. During the worship portion of that first service, there were times when I doubted I would be able to make it through, let alone be able to stand up and walk to the platform. But the moment I took the stage, I sensed the power of God, and I felt calm.

You can watch the message online, but I'll give you the

highlights here.[7] I had brought our Christmas card to the pulpit with me. After I preached that Jesus' birth signaled the end for loneliness, fear, despair, and guilt, I picked up the card and announced my final point. Looking at Lenya's face, I read the verse on the card and then declared that Jesus has turned off the darkness of death too. I then told them what I want you and every human being on this planet to know: you don't have to fear death! It is defeated. Destroyed. It is painful, but there is no power left in it. In fact, for those who know Christ, death itself is a gift, for to be absent from the body is to be present with the Lord (2 Corinthians 5:8).

This is what God wants for you: Forgiveness. A relationship with you. Heaven. Though Christmas is Jesus' birthday, he offers *you* the present, the free gift of eternal life. Jesus left heaven and came to earth so we could go to heaven when we leave earth.

At the end of the message, I gave a simple invitation for people to stand to their feet and pray, to give their hearts to Jesus and receive that gift.

The Bible promises that if you believe in your heart that Jesus is Lord, and confess with your mouth that he rose from the dead, you will be saved. You can pray something as simple as this:

> *God, I believe that I am a sinner. I'm broken, and I can't fix myself. I believe that Jesus is your Son and that he died on the cross in my place. I believe that he rose from the dead. I turn from my sins and turn to you. Please forgive me and help me follow you. In Jesus' name I pray, amen.*

A prayer that basic—or even more stripped down—if prayed in faith has the power to change your heart and save your soul forever. In fact, you could say something like that to God right now as you're reading this book and be transformed from the inside out. If you never have, I pray that you will!

In response to that message, people from all of our campuses across the state of Montana stood and asked Jesus to turn the dark off in their hearts. Amazingly, there were also people who were watching our program on the Internet and listening on the radio who decided to follow Jesus right where they were. What floored us was hearing later that included in those who were present and moved that night were two paramedics who had attended in Lenya's honor.

COMING FULL CIRCLE

Fifteen months after Lenya went to heaven, I found myself back in the middle of the Big Apple. I was preaching at Hillsong NYC, an explosive move of God meeting in the historic Manhattan Center Grand Ballroom, just a stone's throw away from Madison Square Garden. Thousands of people from all walks of life and all five boroughs packed the services I preached at, which began in the morning and went late into the day. The title of the message was the same as the one I preached during the Christmas from hell and that you just read in this chapter: "Turn Off the Dark." While standing backstage waiting to go on, I thought of that moment on Broadway when I looked up at the sign and heard God speak to me. I marveled at his goodness.

Little did I know that one of the actors who plays Spider-Man would be in attendance. He tweeted later, "Wow. This Spider-Man certainly resonated with the incredible message @levilusko brought today entitled 'Turn Off the Dark.' #takeheart."[8]

All my boyhood dreams were now fulfilled. I reread the tweet in disbelief and even Googled the actor's name to make sure it was legit. I had just preached a sermon to Peter Parker that, little did he know, he had helped me write.

FIVE

NO INHALERS IN HEAVEN

It is an honor to have been entrusted with the job of being a daddy to four little girls. Since children are compared to arrows in the hand of a warrior (Psalm 127:4), Jennie and I like to say that we have one in the target and three in the quiver. Occasionally, when I have been out with all the girls by myself, random strangers have approached to give me helpful information like, "That's a lot of kids" or "You're way outnumbered." Thanks? I hadn't noticed. Please, tell me more, should any painfully obvious ideas pop into your head.

When people would see me with two of the girls in a stroller and two walking along, inevitably somebody would crack something along the likes of, "Good luck" or "You poor thing" or some other meaningless token of verbal benevolence. There have also been times when someone has made the mistake of pointing out how frustrating it must be to have not yet gotten the boy that I surely must desire. I have been accused of a lot of things, but having a long fuse is not among them, and I have zero patience for people insinuating in front of my little girls that I see them as stepping stones on the way to the son I really want. I should probably veil my disgust a little better in those moments, but speaking loud enough for my girls to hear me, I always respond that my daughters are amazing and that it is an absolute dream come true to get to be their dad.

Of all the father moments that rock, there is nothing so epic as snuggling in bed once they are tucked in and beginning to get a little drowsy. Notice that I didn't say anything about the process of getting them to that point. That is just madness. Sheer insanity. If you're not yet a parent, know that I'm not exaggerating one bit. The moment you announce that bedtime is drawing near, your kids will collectively lose their minds. Successfully getting four little sets of teeth brushed, bodies bathed, pajamas on, and rpm down is about as manageable as simultaneously riding four bucking broncos. Anyone who tells you different is a liar. Progress you make on one front is immediately challenged by at least one child revolting and undoing all your work. At some point someone will inevitably be running down the hall with underwear on her head, wearing a pair of her mom's high heels. Who just wrote on the wall with that marker, and where did you get that cookie?

Fortunately there is fun to be had even in the height of the craziness: Pajama dance parties with Skrillex as a soundtrack. Crazy stories about talking horses. Discovering your second-born daughter can do the splits perfectly. Plenty of little monkeys jumping on the bed. And once they have calmed down enough after reading books and praying, you get to snuggle them. There is nothing like it in the world: leaning over their beds and giving them big hugs, hearing their little squeals of feigned outrage over the sandpapery scratchiness of my stubble on their smooth skin, and exchanging Eskimo kisses with the tips of their noses tickling mine.

One night I was tucking four-year-old Lenya in, and we were talking about how Jesus is called "Everlasting Father" in Isaiah 9:6. It was just a week before Christmas, and we had been memorizing the verse as a family, adding on a title each day: "Wonderful Counselor," "Mighty God," and so on. I explained that "Everlasting Father" actually means that God is the author of eternity, and I told her how awesome it is that because of this, Jesus can offer us life even after our time ends on earth.

Lenya asked me, "How do we get to heaven?"

Assuming that she was asking about our responsibility to accept the gift of eternal life, I responded, "By believing in Jesus."

She said, "No, how do we *get there*, after we die?" She clearly wanted specifics about the method of transportation, not just the mechanics of salvation.

This stopped me in my tracks. "Well . . . God takes you," I managed.

"Like on a unicorn or on a horse?" she asked.

I didn't know exactly what to say to that; it was too surprising and beautiful to hear her muse so seriously about transit between earth and eternity. No wonder Jesus said you must become like a little one to enter the kingdom (Matthew 18:3).

Since I had not come up with anything helpful, she thought about it for a second and then decided on an acceptable answer to her own question: "Probably on a flying horse." She was clearly settled that this was, in fact, the only logical way the trip could be made.

Then she added, "But if you don't believe in Jesus, you go to jail."

And with that she began to drift off to sleep. Once she was

out, I hurried to write down what she had said before I could forget a word of this amazing conversation.

Exactly one year and two days later, she found out exactly how you get to heaven as she made that glorious journey. Those were panicky moments for us. We were trembling and desperate. Hot with fear and delirious with shock. It was cold, dark, and awful. Not so for Lenya. The same night that was the worst of our lives by far was for her the beginning of endless summer and joy unspeakable. She fell asleep on earth and woke up in the presence of the Father of eternity. While we began to live a nightmare, she had woken up from the dream of this life, and a bright and glorious day was dawning that would never end. Did she ride a flying horse? I won't need to ask her. The next time I see my daughter I will have made the journey myself.

DID SHE RIDE A FLYING HORSE? I WON'T NEED TO ASK HER. THE NEXT TIME I SEE MY DAUGHTER I WILL HAVE MADE THE JOURNEY MYSELF.

THE EASY PART AND THE HARD PART

I have never doubted that Lenya is having a great time. When I think of her on the distant shore of heaven, I imagine exotic, lush, tropical scenery and exhilarating adventures. The word *paradise* informs my imagination. That's what Jesus called it when he promised the thief on the cross a ticket (Luke 23:43). Paradise! Like Maui, Tahiti, or Fiji.

There's nothing I can't stand more than the lame heaven myths that have been endlessly perpetuated by the devil to keep us from looking forward to it. People floating on clouds, everything looking translucent, Gregorian chants playing endlessly on the sound system (probably from off a Zune or a Discman), and—of course—chubby, naked baby angels flitting around. For the record, I have read the entire Bible, and I haven't ever found a mention of a single chubby, naked baby angel.

In fall 2014, *Rolling Stone* magazine interviewed Stephen King, who has spent his career writing about death. When the interviewer asked, "Do you hope to go to heaven?" he responded, "I don't want to go to the heaven that I learned about when I was a kid. To me, it seems boring. The idea that you're going to lounge around on a cloud all day and listen to guys play harps? I don't want to listen to harps. I want to listen to Jerry Lee Lewis!"[1]

That's why it's a mistake to allow unbiblical imagery, perpetuated by cartoons, comic books, and well-intentioned but misinformed Sunday school teachers, to color our thinking.

I am with Stephen King 100 percent. I don't want to go to such a heaven either! Fortunately no such heaven is actually to be found in the Bible.

Heaven is a place, like New York or Paris. Untainted by sin and disease, and unspoiled by evil, it is like earth, only better. Heaven is full of laughter and play, eating and drinking, working and exploring—all infused and energized by the presence of God and pulsating with holy wonder. When I think about Lenya there, I don't picture her looking back longingly at her life here on earth, wishing she could go back, like Uncle Rico from *Napoleon Dynamite*. I see her riding a horse down the beach, her hair whipped by the warm wind, a huge smile across her face. She is living in the midst of her glory days and no doubt is thrilled when she thinks of us getting to join her there.

For me, this is the easy part.

The hard part is dealing with the aftermath on earth. She got to go to heaven, but she left her body here. The body we saw on the screen of the ultrasound and felt kick inside Jennie's belly. The body whose growth we marked as she stood with her back against the pantry door. The nose I kissed with mine. Her tiny hands we held as she learned to walk. Her cute little chin. The bottom lip she would suck on when deep in thought. Her big brown eyes and wild hair. Those little feet we loved to tickle. She went, but her body stayed.

Jennie and I had a very difficult time picking out the clothes to bury her body in. We thought more than a few times that no matter what we picked, Lenya would have modified it. She had style for miles. Lenya would put together outfits for her sisters and loved accessories that, in her words, "popped." When it came to her unique sense of style, she had a very flamboyant, rock-and-roll edge. She would break rules and pair things together that were unexpected, but she pulled it off effortlessly. Our friend Crystal, who sang at Lenya's celebration, said that on a number of occasions she would see Lenya rocking an outfit and wonder if it came in an adult size.

We ended up picking her sparkly red Toms, a flannel over a sweater, and a pair of leggings and a skirt. The funeral home asked for a picture of her hair so they could style it, and we picked a shot where she had her bangs pulled up in a tall pompadour but the rest of her wild mane free. Her sisters approved of the choices, and together as a family we put things in her little purse. This all was unspeakably hard.

Thinking of her little body being buried in the ground in a box nearly caused me to collapse with sadness. In the weeks following, I would almost hyperventilate when I would visit the cemetery or drive by the hospital or funeral home. Any scene in a movie involving CPR, defibrillators, and frenzied lifesaving in emergency rooms was almost enough to induce panic attacks, and they're still very difficult for me to watch. Ambulance sirens give me flashbacks.

In the midst of this heartache, I began to understand why many people turn to drugs or alcohol to dull their senses and shut out the pain when trying to deal with loss. I never really understood those who cut themselves before, but now it made much more sense to me. It's possible to hurt so much inside that making blood run from your arm seems as if it would be a welcome distraction and an area of pain you have control over. Grief gave me greater compassion and sympathy for those bound up in destructive coping mechanisms.

For me, though, instead of wanting to forget or shut it out, I was desperate to learn. I knew that what I was seeing and living was only part of the story. We are not supposed to walk by sight but by faith. I made the decision to look not at just what was in front of me but at what God said was there. I had to study and investigate what God's word has to say about what had taken place. I had to put on the eyes of a Lion.

BREAKING CAMP

I found the greatest comfort in 2 Corinthians 5. Tons of people bought us books about the afterlife and grief and mourning. Some were interesting, and others were awful. In what Paul had to say to the Corinthians, I found something powerful I could sink my teeth into:

> For we know that if our earthly house, this tent, is destroyed, we have a building from God, a house not made with hands, eternal in the heavens. For in this we groan, earnestly desiring to be clothed with our habitation which is from heaven, if indeed, having been clothed, we shall not be found naked. For we who are in this tent groan, being burdened, not because we want to be unclothed, but further clothed, that mortality may be swallowed up by life. Now He who has prepared us for this very thing is God, who also has given us the Spirit as a guarantee.
>
> So we are always confident, knowing that while we are at home in the body we are absent from the Lord. For we walk by faith, not by sight. We are confident, yes, well pleased rather to be absent from the body and to be present with the Lord. (vv. 1–8)

Digging into these verses gave me strength and peace in ways I will never be able to articulate. Paul basically says that this life is a camping trip. Instead of canvas and poles, we are all bivouacking in flesh and blood. But what goes up must come down. The more you use a tent, the more trashed it gets. Paul would know this better than anyone. He was a tentmaker, the old school equivalent of a one-man REI. This skill subsidized his ministry and is why we use the phrase *a tentmaking job* to describe a bivocational minister's other employment. The word *tentmaker* in the Greek literally means "tent repairer." Paul didn't just make new tents; he would patch up beat-up, old ones. Eventually, though, a tent would be irreparable, so the person couldn't use it anymore.

That is death.

No camping trip can last forever. Eventually the fire must be put out and the tent taken down. We all must break camp sooner or later. But, Paul insists, when that happens, all is not lost.

When this tent dissolves, we have a house in the heavens. In the Roman Empire, tents were often used as temporary dwellings while houses were being constructed. When the home was finally ready, you left the cramped tent. The departure was an upgrade.

As agonizing and painful as it can be, death is the ultimate upgrade for the believer: moving from the tent into the home Jesus has been preparing for you. Charles Spurgeon once preached, "Death, as it pulls away our sackcloth canopy, will reveal to our wondering eyes the palace of the King in which we shall dwell forever, and, therefore, what cause have we to be alarmed at it?"[2]

DEATH IS THE ULTIMATE UPGRADE FOR THE BELIEVER: MOVING FROM THE TENT INTO THE HOME JESUS HAS BEEN PREPARING FOR YOU.

The tent that you leave behind is not you. You are not your body. You will never be buried. There is not a single person in a cemetery. Those who used to inhabit those tents have moved on into eternity. Death is not the end of the road; it's just a bend in the road.

I have had to force myself to remember this idea often, especially in the first year after Lenya went to heaven, when the wounds were so raw. I would have dark moments when fear would creep in. I shivered when I stood at her grave, hating that she was buried in the cold ground, and I would feel my courage beginning to slip. In those moments I had to reframe my thinking. I remember one time in particular I literally got out my Bible and preached a little sermon to myself with tears streaming down my face:

"Lenya is not lying there, cold and shivering. Even though her tent was destroyed, she has a house in the heavens, made without hands. When she left the tent, she got to go home, and the house has got what the tent does not. There is no more asthma, or allergies, or sickness, or sin, or death forever. She is with Jesus in paradise, and I am going to see her when my tent is taken down. Jesus is the resurrection and the life, and anyone who believes in him, though they die, they will live."

DEATH WAS NEVER THE END OF THE STORY

When I looked at the situation like that, through the eyes of a Lion, my spine filled with steel. Fear was replaced by faith. Resolving to believe has always been the defining mark of the followers of Jesus, ever since the very beginning of the church. During the plagues under Emperor Marcus Aurelius, a staggering third of the city of Rome died.[3] Mourning and grief were pervasive. People were hopeless and stunned. A historian noted that, in contrast to the prevailing despair, the Christians seemed to carry their dead in triumph.[4] This is how God intends for us to face the grave and why the resurrection of Jesus is of such vital importance. Paul argued that if Christ is not risen, than all of Christianity is undone (1 Corinthians 15:14).

We must fight to remember that the grave doesn't get the last word. The body that was taken from us will be returned in our resurrection. Jesus said, "Do not marvel at this; for the hour is coming in which all who are in the graves will hear His voice and come forth—those who have done good, to the resurrection of life, and those who have done evil, to the resurrection of condemnation" (John 5:28–29).

The very word *cemetery* itself comes from the Latin word *dormitory* and means "sleeping place." When the coffin lid closes it sure seems final, but it is only a temporary arrangement. One day Jesus will give a wake-up call to the bodies in the dorms, and they will rise. This promise is the hardest to remember when you need it the most, but you must force yourself to look at death through this lens.

Jennie and I were terrified when friends drove us to the funeral home to see Lenya's body in her casket before the burial. Part of us didn't want to do it at all. We had been with her when she died, so the whole closure thing was a done deal. We went back and forth on the viewing; on the one hand, we would prefer to remember her alive and not have the image of her body in a casket stuck in our heads. But we couldn't help but feel that we would regret not seeing her. We sought counsel, and in the end we decided to go. I am glad we did.

The car smelled like coffee. Our friends who drove us had lovingly picked up our favorite drinks. As we made the short trek to the mortuary, I opened my Bible and read 1 Corinthians 15 out loud, making the choice to look at this viewing through the telescope of faith. My voice trembled and my hands shook as I read, "The body is sown in corruption, it is raised in incorruption. It is sown in dishonor, it is raised in glory. It is sown in weakness, it is raised in power. It is sown a natural body, it is raised a spiritual body" (1 Corinthians 15:42–44). We would see not only what was there but the invisible too.

We walked into the room where her casket sat with the lid opened. Though it was extremely painful to face, we didn't rely on the naked eye, so we didn't lose heart. This little body, while no longer Lenya, was precious to us and to God. Though it would be sown in dishonor and was seemingly dormant, it was not finished. Lenya's body will rise from the grave, shatter the tombstone, and leap forth, immortal and powerful forever.

The same thing will happen to you. God's endgame for your body is for it to come forth to reclothe your soul, just as an acorn goes into the ground and comes out an oak. Paul promised us exactly that when he said, "As we have borne the image of the man of dust, we shall also bear the image of the heavenly Man" (1 Corinthians 15:49). Just as Jesus' body lay still and cold for three days while he was in heaven (welcoming the thief on the cross into paradise, among other things) before he returned to it and it became glorious, so we will return to our bodies once again.

After the resurrection Jesus wasn't a ghost, and he wasn't in a different body; his disciples touched the nail wounds from the cross that were inflicted on him by Pilate's soldiers. He went to drastic lengths to make sure his disciples saw his wounds and touched him and watched him eat. Why? So the experience would leave an impact on them and so we would know what's in store for us.

The resurrection of our bodies is not immediate, though; there is an interval. From the moment you die until the moment Jesus returns, you will be in heaven but not yet back in your resurrected body (John 14:3–4; 1 Thessalonians 4:13–18). Theologians refer to this period as the *intermediate state*. It's like an intermission between the first and second halves of a Broadway play. During this time those in heaven are having an out-of-body experience awaiting the resurrection.

What is that like, exactly? you are probably wondering. Good question. There is nothing I wish I knew more than this.

Some people think perhaps God grants physical properties

to souls upon entry into paradise. Others theorize that temporary bodies are prepared. We don't really know. There are at least three bodies in heaven, though: Elijah, Enoch, and Jesus all went there physically, so we know it is a location suitable for living with a body (Genesis 5:24; 2 Kings 2:11; Luke 24:51).

However the details shake out, there's no way people in heaven are distressed to be away from the bodies they left on earth. The resurrection of our bodies is not because of necessity but because of desire. It will happen because God wants it to and because he can.

The disciple Peter has been in heaven for two thousand years or so. I imagine Jesus reminding him that he is going to one day live in his body again. I think Peter would find that strange. He was only in his body for forty-some years. He has had the better, heavenly version for much longer. Does it seem odd to Peter that God would be so determined to get his old one back and give it to him?

As a father I understand. Something precious was taken from God's kids, and God wants to take it back—out of principle. Because he loves us he will snatch our bodies from the jaws of the grave. He will take the ashes and dust that were once hands and feet, heart and lungs, and—just as he did in creation—fashion a permanent dwelling place for us out of the particles. He has already planned out a victory taunt for that day: "O Death, where is your sting? O Hades, where is your victory?" (1 Corinthians 15:55). This is about as close as God gets to talking trash!

It is not only comforting to dig into what the Word of God actually declares about these things—it's also invigorating. But if we don't understand what God has promised we will experience unnecessary fear or dread.

⚓ ⚓ ⚓

Several months after Lenya went to heaven, we found a video Alivia filmed that we had never seen. Lenya was wearing a Snow White dress, and Alivia egged her on as she jumped on furniture (that, by the way, she wasn't supposed to jump on) and wildly spun and whirled around the room. Finally, out of juice, Lenya lay down on the ground and said dramatically, "I die."

Believe it or not, this is common behavior for a little girl wearing a Snow White dress. If you haven't seen the movie in a while, this Disney princess eats a poisoned apple that makes her fall into a deep sleep that only true love can awake. She is put into a glass coffin until her prince wakes her up and takes her to a castle, where they live happily ever after.

As we watched the video, tears forming in our eyes, we assumed this part of the story was what Lenya had in mind. But after lying on the ground perfectly still for a few moments, she suddenly stood to her feet and declared, "And get back up . . . with Jesus . . . in heaven!"

Our hearts skipped a beat. The video was filmed five days before Lenya did just that.

People commonly say "Rest in peace" or "RIP" as a final salvo over a grave. God has three different words for you to hold onto in faith as you approach the death of believers. Those three words are "Raised in power!" Because of Jesus, you can be solid as a rock and as immovable as an aircraft carrier until the moment when your own personal flying horse comes to bring you home.

SIX

CUE THE EAGLE

When Jennie and I were in birthing class, the instructor told us about the progression from Braxton-Hicks contractions to early labor to hard labor (though, from the husband's point of view, *all* labor should be described as hard) to transition to pushing, which would culminate in the worst moment, something called *the ring of fire*. That is the point when the baby's head crowns. (I get woozy just typing those words. After giving birth to our first three daughters naturally, with not even an aspirin to dull the pain, my wife decided to have an epidural for the fourth. She asked me what I thought. I told her it was a good call, and I was thinking about having one too.)

While we're on the subject, you ought to stop reading right now, put down this book, and thank your momma. Go on. I'll wait here. She went through the ring of fire for you! The least you can do is send her a text and tell her you love her with a little blowing kiss emoji or something sweet.

When someone you love leaves this world, the grief process

is like pregnancy in reverse. You begin at the ring of fire and move backward. You don't work up to the worst—you start there, gripped by spasms of agony so fierce you cry out gutturally and come physically undone. The prophet Simeon told Mary she would have her soul pierced by a sword (Luke 2:34–35), and that was fulfilled when she stood at the foot of the cross and entered the ring of fire, watching her baby boy die. Nothing can ever be as severe as the initial crushing blow when the person you love is torn from you. It's just blood, sweat, and tears. And Kleenex. Lots and lots of Kleenex. If you ever see a grieving person with little white flecks all over his or her clothes, that's because it's hard to remember to check all the pockets of every article of clothing before washing them, and all those tissues wreak havoc when they end up in the dryer. The struggle is real.

From the ring of fire, you transition into heavy sorrow. The contractions of sadness start out so stacked together, so constant, that it feels like an unending seizure of suffering. As the days give way to weeks, there are moments of respite between these attacks as you learn to breathe and ride them out. This is when you are in great danger of getting knocked down, because while the magnitude of these tremors isn't as intense, you are no longer in shock and can feel more pain. As time goes on, intermittent spikes of trend-defying bursts of pain pop up out of nowhere, followed by periods of relative calm when, like a woman in a birthing room, you can get in a few ice chips.

Will the pain ever end? Not on this earth, no. A mother can experience symptoms at any point in a pregnancy, and distance from pain is no foolproof shield. Fortunately, the symptoms of early pregnancy are usually nausea and fatigue, not teeth-clenching, bone-rattling waves of total-body pain you have to grimace to get through. With grief—the reverse pregnancy—the horrors gradually subside but never go away entirely. How can they? When something is ripped out, there is always a hole. God is good enough to coat the raw and jagged edges in grace, if you will let him. The pain in your life will remain, but like an oyster that covers an unwelcome irritant, layer by layer, to protect itself, we can turn it into a pearl. In time, you will go from waves of sadness so severe that they require every ounce of your concentration just to survive to being able to carry the pain and smile at the same time.

With not even two years of experience under my belt, I am certainly no expert. But I do know that today wasn't as hard to get through as day two was. At some point along the way, I learned to not resist happiness or feel guilty when I felt good. Though it feels like a betrayal, being able to enjoy life doesn't mean you don't miss the person who is gone. If I limp my way to the grave, I'm good with that, but I told God that if he wants to heal my limp, I will not fake one. I have lately been learning to enjoy the bittersweetness and longing I feel when I miss Lenya in the midst of happy moments; instead of simply being sad she is not here, I view those feelings as the proof of my love for her. It builds anticipation for our reunion and secretly pulls her into what is happening here on earth, if only in her daddy's thoughts.

God has taught my heart to sing again, and tucked away in the minor key, I hear his promise of all that is yet to come. I can honor Lenya by dancing and laughing just as I can by crying. There are good days and bad days, good hours and bad hours. For a long time it felt as if I'd take three steps forward and twelve

GOD HAS TAUGHT MY HEART TO SING AGAIN, AND TUCKED AWAY IN THE MINOR KEY, I HEAR HIS PROMISE OF ALL THAT IS YET TO COME.

steps back, an awful real-life game of Chutes and Ladders. From time to time, I still get taken to a very low place by a rogue wave, but in general my emotions have become much more stable.

If you have just experienced an unexpected hardship—a relationship breaking up, a friend betraying you, or having to uproot and move across the country . . . again—the sadness can seem insurmountable in the beginning. It will get better. Maybe today, while the wounds are fresh, the pain hurts so much you can hardly believe you will come to a place where the suffering is under control. I understand. But keep moving. You mustn't be overwhelmed by the immensity of the journey. Focus on your next step and then the next. You are going to make it.

Just as pregnancy has a pleasurable beginning and a painful ending, grief starts with something brutal and ends with something beautiful: heaven. Not only will you become stronger as you continue to fight your way through the process, but you are moving toward the sunrise. The Son of righteousness will one day arise, with healing in his wings. It should encourage you considerably to remember that there is an end in sight—and no, the light at the end of the tunnel is not a train. This trial will not last forever. Paul said if we have hope only for this life we are of all men most likely to be pitied—but we have hope for the next life (1 Corinthians 15:19). We will be reunited with those who have sailed before us to the distant shores of paradise. The hurting will end forever. Jesus will fully and finally turn off the dark once and for all.

SATURDAYS

Today is like Saturday. Yes, Saturday, the day that comes between Friday and Sunday. In my opinion, Saturday lasts way too long.

I know what you're thinking: *What are you talking about, Levi? Saturday rules! When else do we get to sleep in and ride our Jet Skis?* Let me explain.

Between Jesus' burial on Friday and his resurrection on Sunday, there was Saturday. Good Friday is famous and Easter Sunday is awesome, so we understandably think and talk about these two days most often. But in between, there is this day that doesn't get a lot of play.

That Saturday must have been a day of crushing disappointment. It was a time when promises had been made but were not yet fulfilled. Jesus had said he would come back. He had said death wouldn't be the end of the story. He had promised that if the temple of his body were to be torn down, it would be rebuilt. But he hadn't risen *yet*. All day Saturday, Jesus' spirit was in heaven with his Father and with the thief on the cross. But for his disciples, Saturday was filled with nothing but loss. Jesus' body lay dead, decaying and cold. On Saturday, the rock in front of the tomb embodied the death of all their dreams and Jesus' promise of a resurrection seemed absurd. Sunday was coming, but it wasn't there yet.

I'm sure for the disciples, Saturday lasted way. too. long. For some of them, it was too much to handle. Why do you think the two disciples walking away from Jerusalem on the road to Emmaus had such a resigned attitude? "We thought Jesus *was* going to be the one. He sure showed a lot of potential. Oh, well. Party's over." The humor of the story is that they said all this to Jesus, having no idea he had pulled an Arnold Schwarzenegger: he was back (Luke 24:13–24).

We are today living in the spirit of an extended Saturday. We have a living Savior, so we have a living hope. God is like an elephant when it comes to his promises. He never forgets. Jesus will come back. We will get to see our Savior's face. What the enemy has destroyed will be restored. We will walk on streets of gold. I have more life with Lenya in front of me than behind me.

But not yet. It's still Saturday. And sometimes it seems as if it will last forever.

Saturday is

- when a child knows he will meet his dad in heaven someday . . . but right now can only look at pictures.
- when a person with paralysis has the promise of a new body free of wheelchairs and numbness . . . but still has to struggle through years on end in the body she's in.
- when families celebrate birthdays and holidays . . . but feel the weight of the empty chair at the table.

Perhaps for those in heaven, Saturday is in "Narnia time," lasting just a second, since to the Lord a thousand years is as a day and a day as a thousand years (2 Peter 3:8). Maybe when we get to heaven, it will be like going through a wormhole in the movie *Interstellar*, and we will all enter heaven's gates just moments from each other, no matter how many years apart we died. It's definitely a nice thought, but for now there are still sixty seconds to an hour, and when you are in it, Saturday lasts far too long. To borrow language from Alanis Morissette, it's "a jagged little pill."

Our third-born daughter, Daisy, is probably the most sensitive one in our house. She is sweet, thoughtful, and delicate. Not too long ago, my wife was doing devotions with the girls when the topic of problems came up. Jennie asked the girls if they had any problems they needed God's help with. Daisy blurted out her response immediately: "Well, Mom, I have a problem. My problem is that it's taking too long to get to heaven." I feel the same way!

The trouble with Saturday is that we have no clue when it will end. Jesus specifically told us that no one but his Father knows the hour or the date of his return (Matthew 24:36), and none of us knows for certain when our day will come to die, so we have to just trust that Sunday is on its way.

EAGLE ALERT

Part of the reason I wanted to write this book was so you could have my field notes as you navigate through the rugged and uncharted terrain that is Saturday. We're in this together—the space between promise and fulfillment. Living with your heart set on heaven but your feet still on earth is not easy.

There have been a number of things that have been instrumental in our being able to suffer well, and I want to share them with you. You don't have to be grieving to benefit from this information. I believe it will be ammo for the fight as you rise up to fulfill your calling, no matter what difficulties you are facing. Plus, as the advice goes, you should drink before you're thirsty and eat before you're hungry; you never know when you will plunge into pain and careen wildly into crisis. If you aren't presently in a trial, my advice would be to read these next pages *even more* carefully, so that when suffering inevitably rears its head you will be ready.

YOU SHOULD DRINK BEFORE YOU'RE THIRSTY AND EAT BEFORE YOU'RE HUNGRY; YOU NEVER KNOW WHEN YOU WILL PLUNGE INTO PAIN AND CAREEN WILDLY INTO CRISIS.

There's a scene somewhere in the nine hours of the Lord of the Rings films where Gandalf the Grey is about to be killed but is saved at the last moment when an enormous eagle swoops in and carries him away. Something similar happens in one of the Hobbit movies. A bunch of vicious werewolves have the little dude with hairy feet and his bearded dwarf friends trapped in a tree on the edge of a cliff; they're about to fall when a flock of eagles comes and whisks them away to safety. It's beautiful (the eagle, not the hairy feet).

Keep those pictures in your mind, and read this carefully (because the devil does not want you to know this): as a blood-bought child of the King of Kings, you have the right to cue the eagle anytime you need to. Listen to this promise as it appears from the mouth of Isaiah the prophet:

> Even the youths shall faint and be weary,
> And the young men shall utterly fall,
> But those who wait on the LORD
> Shall renew their strength;
> They shall mount up with wings like eagles,
> They shall run and not be weary,
> They shall walk and not faint. (Isaiah 40:30–31)

This Holy Ghost jet pack is exactly what Isaiah the prophet said we have access to. We don't have to send moths out of a glowing magic staff as Gandalf did to call for our assistance either. When our spiritual batteries are running low, all we have to do is wait on the Lord and ask him for strength. God promises that help will flow in response to such a request. And this strength is not something that you *might* need—there's no doubt you will need it. Isaiah said even the *youths* will faint and be weary; the *young men* will utterly fall. Young people are those with the most strength of anyone. They represent the buffest among us. They do CrossFit and P90X and get up the next day like it's no big deal. But what Isaiah is telling us is even *they* will run out of gas.

The struggles and hardships of this life are more than anyone can bear. No matter how thick your skin is, or how many verses you have memorized, or how high your pain threshold is, even the best of men are men at best. Your heart will fail. Everyone has a breaking point. Just look at the lives of those we would consider to be the strongest characters in Scripture.

Take David, the man after God's own heart. For decades, he held on to God's promise that he would become king. But then he gave up and moved to Goliath's native country, where he worked for the Philistine king and fought the wrong battles (1 Samuel 27).

Abraham, the father of faith, had bad days. He once ran away from the promised land and lied about his wife being his sister to protect himself (Genesis 20). Why? He was afraid.

The apostle Paul begged God three times to take away a painful trial that was far too heavy for him to carry (2 Corinthians 12:7–8).

Elijah, the mightiest of the miracle-working prophets, had a total emotional breakdown when a woman cussed him out. He ended up running away from home, hiding under a tree, and wishing for death (1 Kings 19:4).

The prophet Jeremiah got so stressed out that he told God he was never going to preach again (Jeremiah 20:9).

And then there's John the Baptist. Jesus said that he is the best person ever to be born of a woman. He had such a big crisis of faith in prison that he doubted whether he had made the right choice in baptizing Jesus as the Messiah (Luke 7:20).

You can't imagine a tougher group than these guys—if you saw them together you would probably figure they were trying out for the Sons of Anarchy Motorcycle Club—and yet they all ran out of strength. And guess what? So will you. Especially when you are forced to face the endurance sport that is grief. Whether your grief is from the death of a marriage, the end of a friendship, or the loss of a position at work, there will be times, even as a believer, when you are pushed to your limits and beyond.

Yes, we lifted up our hands in the ER and worshipped God when Lenya died. But right there in that room, as Jennie quietly held Lenya's hands, I was so angry that I paced about like a caged lion and thought about tearing everything off the walls. It's true that I went back in to invite the hospital staff to church, and it's true that I preached days later, but it's also true that a couple weeks after that I was at such a low place, stumbling around a semifrozen lake on a subzero night, that I was tempted to just throw myself in. I would drive around by myself and scream until my voice was hoarse. I wasn't mad at God, and I never found myself asking or caring why it happened. I was just very angry *that* it happened.

And then there's the regret.

I failed as Lenya's father when she needed me the most.

I failed at CPR. If only I had done it better . . . deeper . . . faster.

If only I had gotten there sooner and been with her when the attack started.

Was there a heart condition she had we didn't know about?

Why hadn't I insisted her doctor put her on a different asthma medication like the one I take that helps me out so much?

These thoughts would—and sometimes still do—creep up on me with a paralyzing force. I told you I still get dizzy and flushed during scenes where someone is getting mouth-to-mouth and chest compressions. So many movies and TV shows involve scenes with the paddles and someone yelling out, "Clear!" and the close-up shots of the heart monitors either flickering back to life or flatlining. When you have been through those traumatic moments in real life, watching them on TV is like having a scab torn off your heart.

Some memories became the access point for shame, condemnation, and guilt to run amok in my mind and heart. Every harsh word I ever spoke to Lenya during hyperactive moments when I was working on something and should have been more patient with her. Every trip away from the family to speak at an event I should have said no to. The times I ended up on my phone on Family Day. The occasions when I disciplined her with the unnecessary gruffness of an ogre instead of the tender love of Jesus.

In all these situations I found myself running out of strength, my heart failing, my courage draining. "Even the youths shall faint and be weary, and the young men shall utterly fall."

But . . .

"Those who wait on the Lord shall renew their strength; they shall mount up with wings like eagles, they shall run and not be weary."

You gotta cue the eagle. I discovered that, in moments when I was stumbling, if I called on the Lord and strengthened myself in the name that's above every name—the name of Jesus—I could rise from a heap on the floor with renewed power. The Holy Spirit would energize me and give me what it took to keep pedaling through the pain.

Some of these "eagle encounters" were more dramatic than others. Jennie and I both had moments where we found ourselves on empty—and actual eagles showed up. For me it happened one afternoon at the cemetery. As I pulled into the parking lot, my shoulders began shaking, and I sobbed with waves of sorrow. The snow had melted, revealing the strips of sod pathetically trying to pretend they hadn't been torn apart and placed over a fresh grave. I got out of my car. The wind was cold and the clouds gloomy.

Pilots have a name for an out-of-control plane that is in an irreversible spin toward the earth: a *graveyard spiral*. At a certain point the g-forces become too great to pull out, and a crash becomes unavoidable. Warning lights began to flash inside my head that I was in just such a free fall. My soul was corkscrewing in a graveyard spiral. Sinking to my knees, fears flickering at the edges of my mind like so many tiny flames, I didn't feel as if I could believe.

Just then words from Elevation Worship's "Give Me Faith" came to mind.[1] The bridge to this song is based on Psalm 73:26 and declares that though we may lose our strength, God never will. I pounded the ground with my fist and repeated the lyrics over and over again, tears splashing to the earth.

I rose to my feet and lifted my eyes to the sky to see a bald eagle circling the cemetery, wings spread wide like the stinking Fourth of July.

You have got to be kidding me.

I am not superstitious, but that was superspecial. My eyes were opened, and I saw that God was with me and was prepared to be strong in my weakness. I still saw the grave and the sod and felt the wind, but that was no longer all I saw.

God didn't have to do that, and it doesn't always happen like that, but it meant a lot to me in the moment. Like Noah's rainbow that appeared in the sky, the eagle reminded me of the promises of God, and I didn't feel so alone. That experience, coupled with Jennie's eagle encounter, has led to our home being on full-scale eagle alert. We were recently walking through an airport when two-year-old Clover saw a statue of an eagle and yelled out, "Cue the eagle!" at the top of her lungs. Great advice.

TAKE HEART

Jesus said that in this world we will have trouble, but he instructed us to take heart, because he has overcome the world (John 16:33 NLT). It's interesting that he said "*Take* heart," because *heart* is also translated as *courageousness*, so he is saying, "Take courage." We generally think of courage as an emotion or attribute that you either have or don't. Not so. Jesus' command is for you to take it from his hand—as much as you need.

Taking something is an action. It's a choice. Losing, on the other hand, happens on its own, when you're not paying attention. The truth is, your heart will get lost if you let it. If you would *have* heart, you must *take* heart.

David said the same thing in Psalm 27:13–14:

> I would have lost heart, unless I had believed
> That I would see the goodness of the LORD
> In the land of the living.
>
> Wait on the LORD;
> Be of good courage,
> And He shall strengthen your heart;
> Wait, I say, on the LORD!

Belief is the antidote to losing heart. It puts the lens of faith in front of your eyes and gives you access to limitless courage. As we wait on the Lord, our hearts are strengthened, and we see things that are invisible and can then do things that are impossible.

Regardless of what's weighing you down—whether it's a fight you had with your husband this morning, a big assignment at work that is stressing you out, or the fact that you are being bullied at school and harassed on social media—you have the authority to wait on the Lord and call on his name to receive a fresh infusion of power sufficient for the challenges at hand. And that promise is good all Saturday long.

So, remember to breathe (*hee-heee whooo* is what they taught Jennie and me back in birthing class).

And then cue the eagle.

Sunday is on its way.

SEVEN

THERE'S NO SUCH THING AS A WIRELESS ANCHOR

I was lying flat on my back with blood on my chest. The air was full of the pungent and unmistakable mixture of ink and antiseptic spray. The gun buzzed like a demon-possessed bee as it passed over the lines that had been transferred onto my skin. Every few moments it fell silent as the needle drew up fresh ink from a container and a paper towel wiped excess ink and blood out of the way so the work could continue. My pectoral muscle felt as if it were on fire, as if I were being cut and being burned at the same time. My eyes were closed, and the pain was a relief.

After the gun finally switched off and the paper towel passed by for the final time, I stood up and looked in the mirror to see a piece of art on my body—one that will be there for the rest of my life. Directly over my heart, filling up the left side of my chest, was a giant anchor. Bold lines, clean shading. I loved it.

Jennie was up next. Sid, our talented tattoo artist, scaled down and transferred the same artwork onto my wife's forearm before injecting it with indelible ink.

We got the tattoos fourteen days after Lenya's departure to heaven. Before the funeral we had asked an artist friend if she would paint an anchor on the lid of the casket. It came out beautifully. The black anchor popped on the plain white box, transforming it into something Lenya would have dug. The sight of it being lowered into the grave on that snowy day is permanently seared into my memory.

Lenya loved anchors. She had an anchor T-shirt she often wore. She used to have an anchor necklace, but it had been misplaced (as just about everything in our home inevitably is at some point in the course of a normal week). On our last daddy-daughter date before she left, she had told me she wanted a new anchor necklace for Christmas. We had been sitting in Dairy Queen, drinking Arctic Rush slushies, and she wanted to make sure I had plenty of last-minute gift ideas. Also on the list: lip gloss, a camera, Littlest Pet Shop stuff, an iPod, a new Barbie, and turquoise things.

When we chose Lenya's outfit for the burial, we ransacked the house but still couldn't find the missing anchor necklace. Her older sister, Alivia, volunteered an anchor necklace of her own.

The whole celebration of Lenya's life had an anchor theme to it. The staff at our church surprised us by building giant Pinterest-y anchors out of reclaimed barn wood, metal, and lightbulbs, and used them to decorate the stage of our church for the service. Google "Lenya Lusko Celebration" and you can not only see the anchors but also hear Alivia, who volunteered to speak, talk about Lenya for yourself.[1] (Interestingly enough, that video has been viewed more times than any message I have ever preached.)

The symbol of the anchor is powerful because of what it stands for: hope.

The book of Hebrews speaks of "this hope we have as an anchor of the soul, both sure and steadfast" (Hebrews 6:19). That's a game changer. A boat that is anchored can be battered, but it won't be moved. Because of Jesus, we have hope. And because of hope, even in the midst of the worst storms of this life, we have an anchor for our souls.

> BECAUSE OF JESUS, WE HAVE HOPE. AND BECAUSE OF HOPE, EVEN IN THE MIDST OF THE WORST STORMS OF THIS LIFE, WE HAVE AN ANCHOR FOR OUR SOULS.

Hope is a powerful thing. The evangelist Billy Graham said, "What oxygen is to the lungs, hope is to our survival in the world."[2] In *The Hunger Games*, President Snow said hope is the only thing more powerful than fear.[3] I've heard that in Air Force survival training courses, instructors teach something called the "Rule of Threes": In a survival situation you can last three weeks without food, three days without water, three hours without shelter in extreme conditions, and three minutes without air. But you can't make it three seconds without hope.[4]

The most important battle is the one you fight within, in your mind and heart, to not give up. If you give up hope, you won't have the motivation to do anything else in a critical situation. That's a fact backed up by medical science. Dr. Meg Meeker observed, "Physicians can often tell the moment a terminally ill patient gives up hope. Death comes very quickly afterward."[5]

BUT WHAT IS HOPE?

At its most basic level, to have hope is to believe that something good is going to happen. That help is on the way. That it's not over yet, and no matter how dark it seems, there's going to be light at the end of the tunnel. Hope is a confident expectation. A joyful anticipation. An active, dynamic, energizing enthusiasm. When you have hope, gale-force winds can blow and tsunami waves can smash into the hull of your life, but you are buoyed by the belief that the best is yet to come, that brighter days are ahead. Hope quietly tells your heart that all is not lost, even as storms rage. Our hope is a living hope, because Jesus lives forever.

The author of Hebrews also tells us *what* we are anchored to. Spoiler alert: it's heaven. Keep reading in Hebrews 6: "This hope we have as an anchor of the soul, both sure and steadfast, and which enters the Presence behind the veil, where the forerunner has entered for us, even Jesus, having become High Priest forever" (vv. 19–20).

The veil the writer is talking about is the Holy of Holies, God's throne room in heaven, to which Jesus ascended after he rose from the dead. He went there as a forerunner so we could follow in his footsteps after we die.

The word *forerunner* in Greek is *prodromos*. It describes a pilot boat that would go ahead of a large vessel and bring its anchor into a harbor that was difficult to navigate. In the ancient Roman Empire, the port of Alexandria was notoriously dangerous. Large ships would pull up to the edge and stop until a *prodromos* could come and grab the anchor. Once it was taken to shore, the ship could be slowly and safely winched in.[6]

That anchor is Jesus! He ascended to heaven to bring our anchor behind the veil, where it is permanently fixed. He blazed a trail we could follow, taking the sting out of death so that when we follow in his footsteps, all we have to face is its shadow. As we make our way through this life, we are slowly being winched in, inch by inch.

The thing about anchors is that to be effective, they must be attached to something. There is always a connection: a rope or a chain. They aren't wireless and can't be connected by Bluetooth. That connection is every bit as vital as the anchor itself. It doesn't matter how securely that big hunk of metal is wedged into the ocean floor—if you're not tied to it, it's not the least bit helpful. The chain matters greatly.

The wonderful thing about the anchor of the soul is that it, too, comes equipped with a mighty chain. Hope has a rope: the Holy Spirit. Before entering God's presence in the ascension, Jesus promised to send his Spirit to be our helper. He is our great rope that cannot be frayed, the one who has lashed our hearts to heaven. Through the Spirit we have an everlasting guarantee, a down payment on the life that is to come. He is the proof that there is more in store and that death is not the end.

OBJECTS IN MIRROR ARE CLOSER THAN THEY APPEAR

In times of overwhelming sadness, your anchor should strengthen you, but you should also be encouraged by the chain. Lenya is with Jesus and—through his Spirit—Jesus is in me, so there is a direct connection between Lenya and me.

This was a total lightbulb moment in the initial twenty-four hours after she went to heaven. "She is with him, and he is in me." Hope has a rope. In a very real sense, my family and I are holding hands with the One who is holding Lenya.

To help our daughters see through the eyes of a Lion, we would actually act out this idea as a family. I had Alivia stand around the corner in our hallway, where we couldn't see her, and we pretended she was Lenya. I straddled the corner and represented Jesus, holding both her hand and Jennie's, Daisy's, and Clover's hands. "Though you guys can't hold Alivia's hand or see her, you are directly connected to her through me," I explained. This chain analogy gave us great peace and alleviated the "my child is lost in a grocery store" panicky feeling Jennie and I often felt.

Until we see Lenya in heaven, we are connected with her through the Holy Spirit. Through choosing to be filled with God's Spirit, we can feel the cord grow taut. Honoring Jesus and walking in the light reel it in. The more room we give the Spirit to come upon us and control our lives, and the more receptive we are to heaven's signal and guidance, the greater peace we will enjoy, and the stronger the pull of the rope connected to our Savior and those in heaven becomes.

On the other hand, giving in to temptation and choosing to sin puts slack in the line. So how do you get the slack out of hope's rope? How do you feel more connected? You must be filled afresh with the Holy Spirit. It's no mistake that Stephen's glimpse of heaven through an open door before he died came through his communion with the Comforter. Acts 7:55 says, "He, *being full of the Holy Spirit,* gazed into heaven and saw the glory of God" (emphasis added). The more we are filled with the Spirit, the more heaven comes near.

THE GOSPEL ACCORDING TO IRON MAN

There are lots of ways to grow in your relationship with God's Spirit: serving other people, taking a walk and venting to the

Lord, reading the Bible, talking to a friend you can be real with. But I have found that there is nothing so powerful and effective as gathering together with the church.

In the movie *The Avengers*, there is a scene in which Bruce Banner tells Tony Stark that being the Hulk is nothing but a curse, a nightmare. He feels exposed, like a nerve, and sees no good in it. Tony, on the other hand, views being Iron Man as a responsibility.

He puts it this way: "You know, I've got a cluster of shrapnel, trying every second to crawl its way into my heart." He points to the electromagnetic arc reactor in his chest as he continues, "This stops it. This little circle of light. It's part of me now, not just armor. It's a . . . terrible privilege."[7]

I think of this scene often. I'm no Iron Man, but the pain of grief does feel like a chunk of metal seeking to tear my heart apart. If I had been given a choice between the two, I would choose the shrapnel in a heartbeat because, though time has passed, the sorrow is still very severe.

The one thing that brings the most relief, which I look forward to more than anything, is being at my church, Fresh Life—specifically during the singing, but the whole experience is powerful. When I am surrounded by a throng of God's people and we all lift high the name of Jesus, the worship experience is like Tony Stark's glowing arc reactor: the pressure inside my chest is alleviated, and the sharp barb gets temporarily pulled from my heart.

These are also the moments when I feel nearest to heaven, much more than when I stand at Lenya's grave. With my eyes closed, my hands raised, and the music swirling around me, I get glimpses of God's glory that transcend all else. In those fleeting moments, I feel locked in to the frequency of Jesus, and everything else just fades to gray. What happens in God's house on

WHAT HAPPENS IN GOD'S HOUSE ON SUNDAY IS ABSOLUTELY KEY TO MAKING IT THROUGH SATURDAY.

Sunday is absolutely key to making it through Saturday.

Paul said, "It is the God who commanded light to shine out of darkness, who has shone in our hearts to give the light of the knowledge of the glory of God in the face of Jesus Christ" (2 Corinthians 4:6). There is something about the gathering of God's people that enables this glory to be experienced in a fuller way than is possible on your own. As individuals, we are all a part of the Holy Habitation. When we come together, brick by brick, we are more the house of the Lord than we are alone. His Spirit dwells there in power, and he inhabits our praises. We gather so we can glow and then go.

These moments are like little safe harbors, sanctuaries from pain. For those brief moments, suffering isn't welcome and has no choice but to flee from the power of Jesus Christ. In his light, we see light.

Jennie and I have our spot where we worship at church. We stand there together for the singing, and then I usually get up to preach. We have shed more tears and received more strength there than maybe in any other place. I have looked to the floor and seen a puddle of tears at Jennie's feet more times than I can count. When I look up, her hands are raised, and she is locked into the glory of the Lord, taking heart and renewing her courage.

My friend Carl Lentz told us, "It's better to win ugly than to lose pretty. The secret is to keep showing up." There is real truth to that. Don't quit! Scream if you need to scream, cry if you need to cry, but don't let go—because you are going to need what God wants to give you.

PLANTED, PLUGGED IN, PREPARED

A while back I saw a *60 Minutes* special on a free diver named William Trubridge, who goes to extreme depths in the ocean on a single breath. It is incredibly dangerous. He descends 331 feet below the surface—twice the height of the Statue of Liberty—with no oxygen tank! What he does first is crazy. On the surface he gulps and swallows to pack his lungs more full of air than he could through regular breathing. His lungs swell to the size of watermelons. He knows he is going to a dark place and is storing up all he can for when he needs it. By the time Trubridge completes his descent, the pressure squeezes his lungs to the size of oranges.[8]

The transcendent moments in worship where all of God's people are rallied together, praising the Lord, are like those fleeting moments above the depths: a dark, hard week is coming, and you need all the sustenance you can get. Never take for granted the opportunity to breathe deeply when you are surrounded by an atmosphere of expectant faith supercharged by the presence of God.

It is also crucial that you don't wait for a crisis before you get these sorts of rhythms in place. You must train for the trial you're not yet in. The worst time to try to get ready for a marathon is when you are running one.

We made the decision as a family to plant ourselves in the house of the Lord before the bottom dropped out, and as a result, we had the root systems in place when we needed them the most. Lenya lost her first and only tooth at a weekend service at Fresh Life. And I do mean lost it: it's still there somewhere, because she dropped it in the green room backstage when she showed it to me. This makes me smile. She is in God's eternal house in heaven, but the tooth fairy didn't get her one missing tooth—it's in God's house on earth.

Lions are the only truly social cat; their strength comes not from the individual but from the whole pride. That's why the author of Hebrews warned Christians to not fall into the bad habit of missing church (Hebrews 10:25). Satan wants us separated from the pride so we are easier to pick off. David promised those who are planted will flourish in the courts of the Lord, even in crisis (Psalm 92:13), and as the Lusko ladies and I have made the decision to dig our claws in and commit to the local church, we have experienced great power from the pack.

Each week we bring the first and the best of all we make to tithe to God's work and invest in heaven. There has never been a week of our daughters' lives where this wasn't the case. Jesus said, "Where your treasure is, there your heart will be also" (Matthew 6:21). Our hearts were already set on heaven before Lenya went there. The Sunday before she went home, she brought her money from her "Jesus Jar," where she kept her tithes, and put it in the red collection box at church. I love thinking about how that treasure was waiting—pressed down, running over, with divine interest (Luke 6:38)—for her in paradise.

Proverbs 10:25 says, "When the whirlwind passes by, the wicked is no more, but the righteous has an everlasting foundation." Trials reveal foundations, whether sand or rock, but in the middle of a trial is not the ideal time to build one. If you see a tornado coming in the distance and you think, "We should probably dig out a basement or something," then get ready to say hi to Dorothy and the Tin Man, because you are a goner.

Right now is the time to strengthen your faith. *Today* is the day to put down roots in a local church and sew yourself into the fabric of the body of Christ. Sing your guts out to the Lord as a drowning man cries for air, even when you don't feel your need for him. Open your Bible and seek God's face each morning, on both the days you don't get anything out of it and the days when the verses jump off the page. Have family devotions with your kids regularly. Mix it up. Take a prayer walk together, or do a prayer dance. Don't wait. Do it today. Keep your anchor on a short leash.

The creed of the smoke jumpers (an elite group of firefighters that are like the Navy SEALs of firefighting) is, "Do today what others won't; do tomorrow what others can't."[9] Right now you are in training for a trial you're not yet in. Public victory comes from private discipline. If you are willing to do the hard work now, then when dark days come, you will be ready. Your hands will rise to the heavens by instinct. Verses packed with hope will burst out of your heart. You won't even have to think about what to do; your spiritual muscle memory will be honed. You will have people positioned in your life to hold you up and have your back. You will not faint in the day of adversity. Your trial will not be easy or over quickly, but you will get through it. Your anchor will hold within the veil, and one day the forerunner will bring you safely to the other side.

My girls and I have a game we play where they try to get past me. I pretend not to pay attention, but at the last second I reach out, grab ahold, and pull them into a big bear hug. When they try to get away, I sing this little song I made up: "You're all locked up and you can't go anywhere!" Then I tickle them until they squeal.

Having hope is like being safe in the arms of God. No matter where you go or what happens to you, you are covered. You can rest in his love and be able to say:

When all around my soul gives way,
He then is all my hope and stay.
On Christ, the solid rock, I stand;
All other ground is sinking sand.[10]

EIGHT

PAIN IS A MICROPHONE

There is never a convenient place for a medical emergency, but thirty-eight thousand feet over the Pacific Ocean, in a metal tube traveling hundreds of miles per hour, is a very bad location for one. The baby boy was only six months old, and while sleeping in his parents' arms, he just stopped breathing. They desperately tried to wake him, to resuscitate him. They prayed feverishly for God to bring life back into his tiny body. But when the airplane landed in Honolulu, the child was with the angels in the presence of God.

I spoke to the dad on the phone the week it happened. A mutual friend gave me his number, and I offered to give him a call. He told me I was one of the first people he thought of after his son stopped breathing. I had never met him, but he had followed our story and had read things we had written in the aftermath of Lenya going home. He thanked me and said that we had been a template for him and his wife, teaching them how to go through this tragedy. I prayed for him and listened to him, offering any encouragement I could, and then hung up the phone and began to cry.

I cried as I thought of the difficult days I knew lay ahead for that family. But I also cried out of a profound sense of humility and joy that came from knowing my pain had been used to give hope and courage to a desperate man while his son received CPR in the middle of the night on an airplane ride from hell. God used our suffering to bring a blessing to someone else. This is how God rolls. He puts to use what he puts us through.

In chapter 1, my goal was for you to see that you're not ordinary. God has destined you for impact. There are great things he wants to accomplish through you. In fact, as I've been writing this book, my prayer for you has been that your eyes would be opened to see your greatness in Christ. You have a unique and powerful voice, and as long as you have breath in your lungs, there is a microphone in your hands. How you use the platform you have been given is your choice every day.

An unusual way that you have access to amplification is through suffering. A word of caution: this is going to hurt.

THERE WILL BE BLOOD

> SUFFERING ISN'T AN OBSTACLE TO BEING USED BY GOD. IT IS AN OPPORTUNITY TO BE USED LIKE NEVER BEFORE.

Pain is a microphone. And the more it hurts, the louder you get. Suffering isn't an obstacle to being used by God. It is an opportunity to be used like never before.

This truth leaps off the pages of Scripture again and again and again. Joseph suffered for years as a prisoner for crimes he didn't commit, but it only made him louder. In the end he was raised to the right hand of Pharaoh and put in a position to save the lives of his brothers, who had tried to kill him (Genesis 45:5). Esther went through the unspeakably difficult trial of becoming an orphan when both her parents died (Esther 2:7). Yet her adoption by Mordecai set into motion the events by which she would become queen of Persia and prevent a holocaust. David was forced to go on the run, like Harrison Ford in *The Fugitive*, while he was hunted by his lunatic of a father-in-law, Saul. David was homeless, living in and out of caves in the wilderness of Israel, and yet it was in those caves he poured out his heart to God in worship (1 Samuel 23–24, 26). His greatest praise came from his darkest days.

When the apostle Paul was saved, a prophecy was given to Ananias, who had the unique challenge of discipling this recently converted terrorist. God told him that Paul would stand before kings, gentiles, and the nation of Israel and that he would suffer many things for Jesus' sake (Acts 9:15–16). There are two elements there that we must not miss: (1) Paul would be *used powerfully*, and (2) Paul would *suffer greatly*. But I believe those are actually two sides of the same coin that exists within every calling. It would be *while* he was suffering for Jesus that he would do the great things (speaking to the Jews, speaking to the children of Israel, and speaking to kings).

Here's where this concept comes to your front door. Just as Ananias was to tell Paul that he was a chosen vessel, so you are part of a chosen generation. No ordinary child. You are royalty, remember? A unique part of God's forever family. But there's a catch: just like Paul, you will suffer many things on the way to your destiny being fulfilled.

Pain is guaranteed. The Bible says that the rain falls on the evil and the good alike (Matthew 5:45). Part of living on this fallen planet cursed by sin is that trials are inherent.

That's just the way it is.

What about for the child of God? What happens when you give your life to Jesus Christ? The difficulties ramp up to a whole other level.

Jesus said that he wants us to shine brightly. He didn't just say, "I am the light of the world" (John 8:12); he also said, "*You* are the light of the world" (Matthew 5:14, emphasis added). Daniel said that those who turn many to righteousness will shine like the stars forever and ever (Daniel 12:3). Guess what? God wants to make a star out of you. That's wonderful—but as the great theologian Spider-Man said, "With great power comes great responsibility."

The enemy is not going to let you capture his flag without some serious flak. When you stand up as a Christian, attempt to share your faith, and live to see lost people won, you'll invite suffering, persecution, and opposition your way. This is why Paul told Timothy, "All who desire to live godly in Christ Jesus will suffer persecution" (2 Timothy 3:12).

Adversity is going to happen. In fact, it's part of your calling. We're told in 1 Thessalonians 3:3, "No one should be shaken by these afflictions; for you yourselves know that *we are appointed to this*" (emphasis added). Jesus warned his followers that the world hates him, and if you're trying to follow him, the world's going to hate you too.

CRUSHED LIKE AN OLIVE

The Bible calls us kings and priests (Revelation 1:6). An interesting thing that a king and a priest have in common is that, in Old

Testament times, both had to be anointed. They went through a symbolic ritual of being smeared with oil to show that they were set apart for the platform, the microphone they were called to.

A king couldn't take the stage, the mantle of authority of leadership, without being anointed. Priests had to regularly be anointed and consecrated into their service. That's why it's striking that before Jesus, who is both King and Priest forever, went to Calvary, he first went to the Garden of Gethsemane.

Gethsemane means "olive press." Olive oil is made by pressing olives with a giant stone until the oil runs out. Because olive oil was used in the anointing process, olives had to be crushed so that someone could be anointed. There could be no anointing without a crushing.

Beyond the actual ceremonial oil, Scripture says that there in the Garden, Jesus knelt down and was in such agony, under such great pressure, that he began to sweat great drops of blood (Luke 22:44). At Gethsemane we see Jesus being crushed before going to the cross.

The cross was his stage, the nails the proof of his love. He was willing to take up that dreadful microphone, to use the influence he had been called to: "For this purpose I have been sent" (Luke 4:43). But getting there meant first being pressed like an olive.

There are no shortcuts; you simply cannot get to Calvary without going through Gethsemane. You and I have not been called to die for the sins of the world, but we do have a divine assignment, a mission we've been called to fulfill. And to fulfill it we must be crushed; we must be pressed if we are to see it accomplished. We cannot be used in a great way without experiencing pain. A. W. Tozer wrote, "It is doubtful whether God could ever bless a man greatly until He has hurt him deeply."[1] Your calling involves suffering. There's no way around that.

NOTHING IS WASTED

But be of good cheer. There is a connection between the strength of our pain and volume of our voices. Jesus said in John 12:32, "And I, if I am lifted up from the earth, will draw all peoples to Myself." The more we hurt, the louder we become. This is why, though it is tempting, you must not be selfish with your pain. The things God deposits in your spirit in the midst of suffering are the same things that someday other people will desperately need.

When you're going through a trial, it's easy to block out other people who are hurting. You might think, *I can't worry about them. I'm sorry other people have it bad, but I'm just barely coping. I'm hanging on by a thread. I could hardly get out of bed this morning, so I just need to focus on me right now.* No one will blame you. But you are wasting the anointing oil your crushing produced. If you would be willing to step out in faith and serve other people when you're in the fire yourself, you will find a huge boost in volume, because you are plugged into a microphone called pain.

A woman in our church named Rhonda went home to heaven this year after a painful and exhausting fight with cancer. The disease that ravaged her body made every aspect of her life excruciatingly painful. Keeping food down soon became impossible. Normal day-to-day activities we take for granted when healthy became torture. Yet she refused to focus on herself and instead made it her goal to show God's love to those people cancer gave her access to. Her sense of humor and joy was contagious, and it was impossible to get close to her without being blessed.

There are two reasons why your volume gets louder as life gets harder. First, when you're going through a great time of trial, people around you tend to get quieter. Their voices hush out of respect. Smart people walk on tiptoe around hearts that are on fire.

When you're a Christian and you're going through a great time of difficulty, you will notice that those around you who don't know Jesus Christ—especially those you've shared your faith with before—will lean in extra close. Their ears perk up. They want to see if what you have advertised is going to prove true in the product demonstration. You told them that Jesus is the light of your world. Well, now your power has been cut, and they want to see if you can glow in the dark. You've told them that Jesus is the anchor for your soul; he is the solid rock you can stand on. Now everything around you is giving way, and they want to find out if you're going to sink in the sand. If they do see your claims proven true, you'll find a greater willingness on their part to trust Christ in their own lives.

The second reason your volume gets louder when life get harder is because in trials, you can hear God better. Why is this? Because he comes closer! That's what we find in Psalm 34:18: "The LORD is near to those who have a broken heart."

C. S. Lewis wrote, "God whispers to us in our pleasures, speaks in our conscience, but shouts in our pain; it is His megaphone to rouse a deaf world."[2] And the nearer he is, the better we can hear him and the more we can do for him.

You're actually better fit for ministry in the crucible of pain. You have a stronger voice to project and to declare, and it's easier to belt from the diaphragm of your soul when you're hurting. It's counterintuitive, but in the middle of my hardest mess, I've found ministry to be a great strength waiting to be tapped into. It was welling up within me—a greater desire than ever before to tell the whole world that Jesus Christ can turn off the dark—because I experienced it myself. Right there, at ground zero, in the valley of the shadow of death. As hard as it was to claw our way through on hands and knees in those moments, Jennie and I found that when we poured our pain into ministry, whole new levels of usefulness opened up. There's perhaps no time you are as powerful as when you minister in the midst of pain.

Plus, hard times are a passport that gives you permission to go places you wouldn't get to any other way. Pain can open doors that would otherwise remain locked. There are avenues of influence. There are situations and opportunities you will stumble upon that would never have been yours had things gone well. Interactions, conversations, moments of great usefulness you probably never would have seen had it not been for the chemotherapy, doctor's visit, or trip to yet another rehab facility to pick up your son.

HARD TIMES ARE A PASSPORT THAT GIVES YOU PERMISSION TO GO PLACES YOU WOULDN'T GET TO ANY OTHER WAY.

Jesus articulated this perfectly in John 12:24, when he said, "Most assuredly, I say to you, unless a grain of wheat falls into the ground and dies, it remains alone; but if it dies, it produces much grain." Think about it: going into the ground and dying is not great for the grain. It's a bummer. But the difficulty causes what emerges from the ground to be wonderful.

I love sunsets, but I love sunrises too. I love them more than ever before now that my daughter is in heaven. (Sometimes when they are extra wild, we look up and joke that Lenya was able to help.) And I've noticed something: it's the cloudy, stormy days that produce the best sunsets. Clear days are more fun, but the stormy ones serve a purpose. They give the potential for a killer show in the sky.

A DOOR UNLOCKED

I told you earlier about how my wife told me to invite the people who worked in the emergency room to come to church on Christmas Eve. She saw what I hadn't. The microphone called pain was waiting to be seized. Later we received a note at our church from a respiratory therapist I invited, a woman who also happened to be married to the doctor who had tried to resuscitate Lenya but had told us he was unable to do anything more. This is what she wrote:

> I was not sure where to comment about my wonderful experience with your church! I was invited to go to the Christmas celebration by Levi after the passing of Lenya. I was working the night she came in to the ER. It was by far the hardest thing I have ever been through. That little girl touched my soul and I knew I could not turn down her invite to listen to her daddy preach.
>
> I have not been to church in years. I grew up Lutheran and did all the formalities that go along with growing up Lutheran. I always had so many questions about the Bible, Jesus . . . none were ever answered. I think my confirmation teacher just wanted me to sit and listen. This is the biggest reason why I never returned after starting a life of my own!
>
> My boys, twelve and nine, thought it would be a great idea to all go to Skull Church on Christmas. After I told them that Levi invited me through the spirit of Lenya, we were all very excited. I knew it would be difficult. Difficult is not the word I would use to describe sitting in

the seat, standing to sing with the wonderful band, and listening to the most moving sermon I have ever heard. Levi's words went through my whole body . . . in and out. So many questions were answered. I have never felt so good about listening to someone speak of the Lord before. I just stared at him preaching, and I felt comfortable.

I am still thinking in my head how I understand life and death more now than I ever have before. Before it was more on the medical side. People pass on, but kids should not. Now I am able to understand and feel semi-okay with a child leaving earth and going to heaven. I have never felt that before. I feel a bit ashamed, maybe even lost as in my youth and not understanding where my faith really was. Levi's words laid it out for me. I finally understood so many things I thought I never would. I was deeply moved! Levi is a true inspiration.

I could go on and on about how I felt, what I learned, and what I hope for now from this point on. I really want to say thank you for everything. Levi, you and Lenya have changed me and it feels so good. I feel a lot less frustration after your Christmas service. Thank you for sharing your faith with me, Levi and Jennifer—my husband (ER MD) and I will always have Lenya in our hearts. He wanted me to pass along that he is constantly thinking about all of you. He wishes he would have been able to be there Christmas Eve.

Thanks again. You all are doing an amazing job!

Holly

Not every opportunity to minister through pain will be so dramatic, and many times we will not know the outcome until we get to heaven. But every time we hurt and look not just at ourselves but also at others around us, there are opportunities to be used by God. I never would have walked into a hospital that night to invite strangers to come to church, but my pain became a passport into that place. The door of circumstance was unlocked by the key of difficulty, and I dare you to look at the hardships you're facing and believe that through them, there are people you are meant to reach.

IMPOSSIBLE PAIN, INCREDIBLE POWER

There is also an enormous amount of good that comes to you when you let God flow through you. It doesn't make the pain stop, but it does help your heart heal. No, it's not always easy to jump on the phone with a grieving dad or a mom whose daughter was just killed in a car wreck. Sometimes I would just as soon not go there, knowing it will dredge up painful emotions and memories. But every time I have pushed through and let God use my pain, I have been glad I did—not just for any help it brought to those who suffered the loss, but also for the peace it brought my own heart.

When I am tempted to be selfish with my pain, I think about those who used their trials as occasions to be a strong testimony to me. I think about Pastor Greg Laurie, who was the first person I wanted to talk to on the phone after Lenya died. His own son, my friend Christopher, was killed in a car accident not too long before, and he and his family—at a great emotional cost to themselves—allowed us to follow in their footsteps of grief toward healing. They flew to Montana on Christmas to stand in the snow with us and have been an enormous, indispensable template for us. I can't imagine having gone through this situation without them, and I can't help but want to be that resource for others who are hurting.

God trusted me with this trial for a reason, just as he saw fit to give you your cross to bear. And the more impossible your pain, the more incredible the power he will bring out of it. It's his ratatouille—his specialty, a signature move that he has mastered. I heard someone once say that God gives his toughest assignments to his most trusted soldiers.

It is an incredible honor to be trusted with pain. My spiritual big brother, Steven Furtick, spoke this truth over Jennie and me just two days after Lenya was taken from us. He said words I will never forget: we had been given this mantle for a reason, and he believed God would use us to teach our generation how to suffer. Iron Man was right: it is a terrible privilege.

God doesn't cause bad things to happen, but he is sovereign, and nothing happens outside his permission. The devil is the one ultimately responsible for evil. Sometimes it seems that life is out of control and more is given to us than we can bear. But everything is under God's control, and he leads us to breakthrough when we worship, no matter what we're going through. His endgame is to sabotage all your suffering and use what was meant for evil to accomplish his purposes. He has the devil's credit card number on file and is more than able to make him pay for the damage he does.

You need to actively be on the lookout for every way you can redeem the hell you are put through by shining your light in the darkness. Your suffering is being used to create the anointing oil for the next level God wants you to reach. Squeeze every drop out of your trial. Let nothing be wasted. Hold nothing back. None of your tears have fallen to the ground unseen. God has a plan to put each of your difficulties to use like a seed that goes into the ground and brings forth a harvest of righteousness. I also want you to believe in Jesus' name that there will come a day when the devil will regret ever asking God's permission to give you your trials, because you will end up twice as blessed as you started out.

God wants you to shine brightly. He wants you to reach more people. He wants you to take more ground, and the only reason he has allowed you to be doubled over in grief is so he could pick you up and help you reach new levels of influence you never could reach otherwise. God's up to something! He's turning your mess into a message. He's turning your pain into a platform. He's turning your trial into your testimony and the trash that has come into your life into triumph!

GOD'S UP TO SOMETHING! HE'S TURNING YOUR MESS INTO A MESSAGE.

SIGHT FOR THE BLIND

Our great joy has been seeing Lenya's life and departure to heaven being used by God to touch lives all over the world. God even provided me with a microphone to share the gospel with the people Lenya gave her eyes to. Out of the blue one day, the organization that facilitated the cornea transplants wrote to let us know that she had restored sight to a fifty-four-year-old woman and a fifty-four-year-old man, each of whom had received one of Lenya's corneas. They also told me I could write them a letter. It was emotional for me, but I realized that there is no other reasonable way I would ever get to share Jesus' love with these two people. They now see life through the eyes of Lenya Lion, and as her dad, I have the responsibility of sharing the good news with them on her behalf.

I still haven't heard back from them—and maybe I never will—but I am going to end this chapter with what I wrote to them. I challenge you to be creative and pray about the people you are opened up to reach through your microphone called pain.

Tuesday, July 9, 2013

Hello,

My name is Levi. I have been meaning to write this letter for six months, but I have found it very challenging. On December 20, 2012, just five days before Christmas, our daughter Lenya (five years old) died suddenly and unexpectedly after having an asthma attack. We were completely blindsided.

That night we were asked if we were willing to donate her corneas. It was a very difficult and emotional decision but one that we decided she would want us to make. She was an extremely tender and compassionate little girl with a heart full of love for others. We were very happy to hear that because of her eyes, your vision has been restored. It blesses us to think that just as she saw through those corneas while she was on earth, someone else continues to see who couldn't before.

I wanted to let you know a little about the little girl who gave you the gift of sight.

She was spunky and full of fire. One of her nicknames was Lenya Lion, because of her wild spirit. She loved dancing and music and playing with her three sisters. She was coordinated and extremely good at ballet, swimming, and climbing. She still had training wheels on her bike but was about to begin riding with two wheels. She had just started kindergarten.

More than anything else she loved God. She believed in Jesus and trusted him as her Lord. She understood and was thankful for Jesus' death on the cross and his resurrection from the dead. Though we miss Lenya so much, we know that she is in heaven, and we will see her there again. We can't wait. And just like she was an organ donor for you, Jesus Christ came to earth to lay down his life so that anyone who believes in him might be forgiven: "For God so loved the world that He gave His only begotten Son, that whoever believes in Him should not perish but have everlasting life" (John 3:16). Because of the connection we have with you through Lenya's eyes, our hearts' desire for you, if you haven't already, is to know and see the same love that she experienced through Jesus.

In awe of him,
Lenya's dad

NINE

HOMESICKNESS: AN ACHE YOU CAN'T SHAKE

The soldier had the window seat; I had the aisle. Both of us had been upgraded to first class. Soldiers in the airport always make me emotional—something about seeing the uniform and wondering where they are going and who misses them back home. My heart skips a beat and, knowing they do what they do on my behalf, I want to thank them, but I always feel like a moron.

The soldier's buddies harassed him on their way to the back of the plane:

"Cushy seat, bro."

"Rough gig, but I guess someone's gotta do it."

"Send some drinks back to the cheap seats."

There were more than two dozen soldiers on our flight, a bunch of brave men and women who were serving our country, defending our freedom, and literally putting their lives on the line for the rest of us. Trying hard not to sound stupid, I introduced myself to the one sitting next to me, and said, "I just want to say thank you."

He was headed home, to Houston, Texas, and he was very excited to get there. I knew this because he kept repeating himself, over and over: "I just can't wait to go home."

"We were in simulated combat conditions," he told me at one point.

Like a little kid, I was intrigued. "What does that mean?"

He said, "We were in pretend camp for the last month. We were in California somewhere, but we were pretending to be in Turkey."

I asked a million questions. Basically, for thirty days they were in an area set up like wartime Turkey. I made the mistake of saying, "Did you get an In-N-Out burger? You were in California, after all." He gave me a look that said, *I ate Meals Ready to Eat for thirty days in California. I'm leaving without an In-N-Out burger. Thanks for bringing it up.*

He told me they had to pretend as though they were camping in a combat zone. It seemed awful. He and his partner had to make a tent using their ponchos and the cord they'd been issued. He said it got down to twenty or thirty degrees Fahrenheit at night. All they had were sleeping bags and their makeshift tent, and they weren't in their winter uniforms. Apparently they were pretend camping in summer Turkey, but it was most definitely winter wherever they were in California. He said it was so cold that just touching his M16 would burn his hands, because he didn't have gloves on.

He must have repeated six times different versions of, "I just can't tell you how glad I am that that's over, and I'm finally getting to go home for a little while."

We had a great conversation. By the end of the flight, he had downloaded the Fresh Life app on his phone. I told him how people all over the world watched and listened to our church services online. A Christian himself, he was excited to be able to go to church on his mobile device no matter where he was deployed.

We got off the plane together and parted ways. Just past security I saw him meet up with his family. His sister, dad, and mom were there. They were hugging. His sister looked so proud of her brother in uniform.

His dad instinctively grabbed his son's carry-on. On the flight, the soldier had told me that before joining the military, he had worked with his dad in the oil business. From the father's appearance, I could tell he was a hardworking, salt-of-the-earth guy. His hands seemed calloused and strong. He wore dirty jeans and steel-toed boots. There was a look of pride and a glow about the entire group as they walked with their soldier toward the baggage claim area.

My bag must have passed me four times at the carousel because I couldn't walk away. I just stood there watching, fully creeper-stalking on their happy little moment.

I couldn't help but think I was seeing a real-life version of the camping analogy from 2 Corinthians that we talked about in chapter 5. Read it again:

> For we know that if our earthly house, this tent, is destroyed, we have a building from God, a house not made with hands, eternal in the heavens. For in this we groan, earnestly desiring to be clothed with our habitation which is from heaven, if indeed, having been clothed, we shall not be found naked. For *we who are in this tent groan*, being burdened, not because we

> want to be unclothed, but further clothed, that mortality may be swallowed up by life. (2 Corinthians 5:1–4, emphasis added)

For the believer, death is the permission to put off the poncho, and the cold, and the MREs of this earth. As joyful as life can be, as much as we're thankful for all that God provides for us, it's nothing compared to what awaits us in heaven. And deep down, in the secret recesses of our soul, we know that and subconsciously crave the transcendence of heaven more than anything else.

As that soldier ached for Houston, we desire heaven. This longing is what causes each of us to be on the quest we have been on since birth. It's a hunt for happiness. A search for satisfaction. We all have an ache we can't shake. There's a groaning, a longing, as though the world were not enough.

HARDWIRED TO CHASE HEAVEN

Heroin has been in the news a lot lately. This nasty drug has flared up as a massive problem again in America, more aggressively than at any time in the last fifty years. Actor Philip Seymour Hoffman's tragic overdose in 2014, when he was found in his Manhattan apartment with a syringe hanging out of his arm, brought the drug to the forefront of national attention. He made the news, of course, because he's famous. But many, many people just like him are found dead every day of heroin overdoses. In New York City alone, there was an 84 percent increase in heroin-related fatalities in two years.[1]

But the heroin epidemic is not just in the big city—it's all over America, especially in rural parts of the country. *USA Today* reported that in some communities, opiates now claim more lives than violent crime and car accidents do.[2] The National Drug Threat Assessment ranked heroin as the second greatest drug risk, right after the abuse of methamphetamines.[3] *Breaking Bad*'s Walter White is still in the lead, but he can hear heroin's footsteps.

Heroin is so dangerous because one out of four who try it once will become addicted—*one out of four.*[4] That's staggering. Try it one time, and *boom*, you'll crave it for life.

Rolling Stone ran an article called "The New Face of Heroin," which pointed to a generation turning from OxyContin to heroin as the next logical step of choice. "Oxys" have become very difficult to get, while heroin is cheap, relatively easy to come by, and delivers a similar high. It is also a stone-cold killer.

Rolling Stone interviewed a girl named Eve, a farm girl who grew up riding horses and had posters of ponies up in her room. At the age of twelve, she plunged down the rabbit hole of drugs, taking an Oxy for the first time. The article described her experience:

> She swallowed one. The sensation it produced was more seductive than anything she had ever felt: Home, she thought. This is home. "I could be alone with myself," she says, "and not freak out."

I've heard other addicts describe the sensation as being under a warm blanket: safe and comfortable. Peaceful.

It was not long before Eve moved on to heroin, something she never would have imagined herself doing. Heroin quickly became her sun, and everything else in this young girl's life became planets, overpowered by its gravitational pull. Her friends finally knew there was a problem when she started neglecting her horses, something she never would have done otherwise.

She says, "You can never ever re-create that first rush, but the whole time you're using, you're chasing it." She became addicted to heroin, and her life turned into a living nightmare.[5]

It's no mistake that Eve equates that first high, that rush that she's constantly chasing but never able to find, as being home. All of us have been hardwired to pursue eternity, to chase heaven, our true homeland. As Randy Alcorn, the Yoda of all things related to heaven and the author of many books that gave Jennie and me great peace when Lenya went home, put it in a talk I heard: "You have been made for a person and a place. That person is Jesus, and the place is heaven." Until you're tapped into that knowledge, your heart will be restless.

> IF YOU'RE ALIVE ON THIS EARTH, YOU DESIRE JESUS, WHETHER YOU RECOGNIZE IT OR NOT.

That's why the Old Testament book of Haggai describes Jesus as "the Desire of All Nations" (2:7). It doesn't matter what country or what period of time you live in. If you're alive on this earth, you desire Jesus, whether you recognize it or not. Jesus is the answer to the ache within.

GROANING: THE SOUNDTRACK TO OUR HOMESICKNESS

Billy Graham is without question the greatest evangelist in recent history—maybe of all time. Jennie and I had the honor of meeting him at his home. By providence the e-mail inviting us to come for this epic opportunity came from Billy's grandson Will the morning after Lenya went to heaven, when we were in shock and before hardly anyone knew what had happened.

Receiving this invitation was just one special way God let us know we weren't alone.

There in the mountains of North Carolina a few months later, we sat at his kitchen table and talked about how much we all looked forward to being with Jesus. When we walked in, he was in the middle of deciding between covers for his soon-to-be-released book that was at the time going to be titled *Salvation*. He told me that was what his whole ministry has been about—salvation. We told him about Lenya, and he reminisced about his beloved wife, Ruth, who beat him home. One thing he said that has stuck with me is that if he had it to do all over again, he would have preached more on the resurrection of Jesus. We held hands and prayed together. It was such an unforgettable moment in time, and I will treasure it always.

I have read that when Billy would go out on the massive crusades he conducted around the world, he would be gone for months at a time. Often Ruth would remain back at home, raising the kids. She would miss Billy so much that she would sometimes sleep with his suit jacket just so she could have the smell of him in their bed.[6] Heartwarming. She was just so sick for him to be home.

Someone once asked her if it was worth it, if she wouldn't rather have married someone who would belong more to her than to the world. Ever the pistol, she reportedly shot back, "I'd rather have Billy Graham six months out of the year than any other man on earth for all twelve." (Drops mic, walks off stage.)

The most homesick I've ever been was on a preaching trip to South Korea, when Alivia was two years old and Jennie was nine months pregnant with Lenya. More than a year before, I had agreed to go, but when it came time to leave, I didn't want to, especially with Jennie pregnant. It was a great opportunity to preach the gospel in another country, and it was amazing to see people come to know Jesus, but the whole time my heart was back with my wife and daughter. When we finished I was grateful to finally be heading home. I boarded the plane that would take me to Montana—a flight that included a stopover at LAX. Right as we landed, the entire passport immigration computer system for all of Los Angeles International Airport—one of the largest airports in the world—went down, and airline officials wouldn't let the passengers of any international flights disembark until it was up and running again.

After the nine-hour flight from Asia, we had to stay in the plane for another six hours. We just sat there on the tarmac. It was not awesome. The captain kept saying, "We're going to have you off at any moment." It was torture.

I missed my connecting flight home, of course, because there's, like, one every month to Montana, and the dogsled had already gone. The airline lost my luggage too. But I didn't even care at that point. You can keep my bag. You can take away my citizenship. I don't care what it takes, or whom I have to hurt. I wanted to get home to my daughter and my wife. If John Candy had pulled up in a yellow moving truck full of polka players, I would have gotten on and told Kevin McCallister's mom to scoot over.

There's a technical term for what I was feeling: *nostalgia*. *Nostos* is the Greek word for "return home," and *algos* means "pain." Return home + pain = discomfort you feel when longing to get back to your home. Nostalgia is a bittersweet longing for the past, the sentimental, wistful feeling you get thinking of happy days gone by. It's wanting to recapture something you once had or once felt, some point in your life that was a golden time. It's the way you feel watching a certain movie at the holidays or baking something from a recipe your mom used when you were growing up. It's the pictures you post on Instagram on Throwback Thursdays.

Nostalgia is also big business, because old can be spun as vintage, which can be commoditized. From throwback branding on soda cans and boutique stores selling your granddad's clothes with tags waiting for Mackelmore to pop, to ironic, kitschy brands and products from your childhood that fill the shelves of Urban Outfitters, a lot of money is passed around through the evoking of forgotten memories.

I read that because of social media and how short our attention spans are, nostalgia has been accelerated. Things go from "current" to "classic" much faster than they did for previous generations. It once might have taken decades for nostalgia to kick in; now things are "in" and then "out" and then quickly cycle back as "old school." You'll see something and go, "Man, I remember that!" Uh, yeah—that's because it was only ten years ago!

What's funny is that when you revisit the places from your childhood that you're homesick for, they're almost always a letdown. There is some truth to the adage, "You can never go back." The home you lived in as a kid will seem a lot smaller and older than you remembered it. The video game system you loved was upgraded for a reason. Things often are rosier in the rearview mirror. Besides, the pot of gold at the end of the rainbow of nostalgia is impossible to catch.

The interesting thing about spiritual homesickness is that it's not actually a desire to go back to a place where we used to live. It's an aching for a place where we will live one day. What we have is a case of *future* nostalgia: we're homesick for a place we have never been. The ache we can't shake can find its fulfillment only in heaven. That's why the apostle Paul said, "For we who are in this tent groan, being burdened, not because we want to be unclothed, but further clothed, that mortality may be swallowed up by life" (2 Corinthians 5:4).

> WHAT WE HAVE IS A CASE OF *FUTURE* NOSTALGIA: WE'RE HOMESICK FOR A PLACE WE HAVE NEVER BEEN.

To *groan* is to sigh with anxiety or to yearn. It's a heavyhearted moan. Groaning is the soundtrack to our homesickness, a mechanism to keep us from settling down. It's there to keep our hearts set on pilgrimage and our feet moving forward. It's caffeine for our souls to prevent us from being lulled into sleep. It keeps us alert. Focused on our calling. Laying up treasure in heaven.

We aren't the only ones groaning, either. Romans 8:22 says all of creation groans, eagerly waiting for the revealing of the sons of God. The *whole earth* is groaning: every squirrel, sapling, stream, sunset, and seahorse is bucking and bellowing, twisting and moaning, because things aren't as they are supposed to be.

WRECKED—AND RESET

Did you see the Disney movie *Wreck-It Ralph*? It's awesome. It was the last movie I ever saw in the theater with Lenya, so it remains very special to me. I remember all through the movie I looked over and watched her watch the film. There was such a focused joy and amusement on her face. Lenya had this thing she did during movies: when she found something funny, she would repeat it out loud to herself with a huge laugh and then look up at us. One of the main characters, a little girl with bright eyes and wild hair, reminds us of her.

The movie shows what happens to video game characters when no one is playing them, as in Pixar's *Toy Story* movies. All the characters from the various games hang out together when the arcade is closed. One is Ralph, a conflicted bad guy from the game "Fix-It Felix Jr." He ends up in this other game called "Sugar Rush," a go-cart racing game where everything is sweet: gumdrops, lollipops, candy canes, and all that. The monarch who presides over this land of candy is named—wait for it—King Candy. Everything in the game seems perfect, but you start to realize that something's not quite right. It turns out that King Candy isn't the true king at all. He's really this sinister figure named Turbo, who sneaked in from a different game and messed with the code.

Turbo infected the whole system. Everything got warped, twisted, and, in Ralph's words, turned into "a candy-coated heart of darkness." The rightful ruler is this girl named Vanellope von Schweetz. Turbo usurped the crown and erased everyone's memories, making Vanellope an outcast.

Ralph makes friends with Vanellope. He is a misunderstood giant with a tender heart, and she is a feisty little fireball who has had to learn to be tough to survive. Though she is mocked by the other girls and called a "glitch," she is actually the princess. Working together, the unlikely duo inadvertently discovers her true identity. Behind her moniker, "the glitch," is a clue to the jig that Turbo is running. If Vanellope can just cross the finish line in the go-cart race, the system will be reset to how it is supposed to be.[7]

These are themes ripped straight out of the Bible, by the way. Like the corrupt system in the movie, all the code here on earth has been compromised. When Adam and Eve fell, you could say we went Turbo. The world is cursed. Thistles, tornadoes, venom, cancer, deformities, atrocities, and war—it was not supposed to be this way. All creation is groaning. Of course, it's not Felix who can fix it, but Jesus Christ. His kingdom will come, his will will be done, on earth as it is in heaven (Matthew 6:10). When that happens, the usurper, Satan, will be dethroned. Instead of a golden hammer like Fix-It Felix Jr.'s, Jesus will rule with a rod of iron as King of Kings, and no one will be able to stop him.

At that time, the sons of God and daughters of God will be revealed. We will all rule and reign with him on this reset system. The book of Revelation basically is the Lord's promise to take the video game out of the system and blow the dust off it to clear out the bugs. "The elements will melt with fervent heat," and God will create "new heavens and a new earth in which righteousness dwells" (2 Peter 3:10, 13). When we cross the finish line, all will be made right.

THE BOOK OF REVELATION BASICALLY IS THE LORD'S PROMISE TO TAKE THE VIDEO GAME OUT OF THE SYSTEM AND BLOW THE DUST OFF IT TO CLEAR OUT THE BUGS.

LEAN IN TO THE GROAN

Until then, we groan. Sometimes it's all we can do. When I think about Clover not having memories of her sister because she was just a baby when Lenya went to heaven: groan. When I see Lenya's pink bike in the garage with her helmet dangling from the handlebars, and I realize I can't take her out on a ride: groan. When I think of Lenya not being there to be the maid of honor in Daisy's wedding: groan. When Alivia asks if Lenya's body still has skin or is bones like in pirate movies, a groan is the only way to deal with it. It's the sound of Saturday.

Keeping all of that in mind, read Romans 8:19–22:

> For the earnest expectation of the creation eagerly waits for the revealing of the sons of God. For the creation was subjected to futility, not willingly, but because of Him who subjected it in hope; because the creation itself also will be delivered from the bondage of corruption into the glorious liberty of the children of God. For we know that the whole creation groans and labors with birth pangs together until now.

The phrase "earnest expectation" is key. If you translate it directly, it means "to stand on your tiptoes and crane your neck."[8] I know full well what this looks like. All four of Jennie's and my daughters are little ballerinas. From the moment they learned to walk, they would almost constantly prance around our home on their tiptoes. I honestly can't ever remember Lenya walking flat on her feet. She almost bounced with energy and was up on her toes from the moment she woke up until she fell asleep. With the phrase "earnest expectation," Paul is saying that the whole world is so full of edge-of-your-seat excitement concerning the return of Jesus and the glory that will be unleashed that it can't contain itself from being on tiptoes in anticipation.

And guess what? There is no greater help to holy living than leaning into that groaning by fostering your future nostalgia. You must make the choice to live on your spiritual tiptoes, setting your mind on things above, not on things of this earth. The future is where you must focus, not the past. It makes my stomach sink to think of that dark day in December, but it makes my heart soar to think of *that* day—the glorious one we wait for, when the Lion shall appear and my little Lenya Lion with him. When your heart is properly focused on the things that are to come instead of paralyzed by the hard and the horrible things you have had to handle, you are postured to be effective in the present.

Earth is not your home; heaven is. And when we arrive on that distant shore we won't have to groan anymore. We will be home.

C. S. Lewis's Chronicles of Narnia series ends with many of the characters in the country of Aslan the Lion, where they find they can run as fast as a horse without being tired, reunite with friends, and eat fruit that makes the juiciest peach in our world seem like wood. Aslan observes,

> "You do not yet look so happy as I mean you to be."
>
> Lucy said, "We're so afraid of being sent away, Aslan. And you have sent us back into our own world so often."
>
> "No fear of that," said Aslan. "Have you not guessed?"
>
> Their hearts leaped and a wild hope rose within them.
>
> "There *was* a real railway accident," said Aslan softly. "Your father and mother and all of you are—as you used to call it in the Shadowlands—dead. The term is over: the holidays have begun. The dream is ended: this is the morning."
>
> And as He spoke He no longer looked to them like a lion; but the things that began to happen after that were so great and beautiful that I cannot write them.[9]

Take a walk. Look at the stars. Watch the sunset. Turn off the TV and gather with your family in front of a fire instead. Listen to creation sing to King Jesus. Take a big, deep sigh. Let your worship and your pain swirl together and become a holy moan.

David said, "Deep calls unto deep at the noise of Your waterfalls" (Psalm 42:7). There is a sympathetic resonance that happens when the groaning is in stereo. It's not just your heart and all of creation you're hearing; the Holy Spirit himself groans in our hearts, reassuring us with sounds that can't be uttered that we belong to God and we are bound for heaven. It's the Lion's roar you're feeling deep down in your soul.

Turn up the groaning. Ratchet up the nostalgia for your future home at every opportunity. Foster excitement for all the joy and glory that await. To the degree that you cultivate your sense of longing for the next world, you will be able to combat the deadly hypnotizing pull of this one.

TEN

PANEM ET CIRCENSES

Alivia was eyeing my Coke. Maybe she was trying to play it cool, but her craving was written all over her face. Two-year-olds have a lot of virtues, but subtlety isn't generally one of their strong suits. She had her own juice right in front of her, but once she heard me crack open the can, her sippy cup lost its appeal. We were sitting on bar stools at the kitchen counter, and I watched her stare at my soda, completely mesmerized by it. I probably would have just given her a drink—my way of overreacting to the strict health food diet I was raised on—but Jennie had assured me that it really isn't good for toddlers to drink Coke.

"How's that juice, Liv?" I asked.

"Good," she responded, without so much as even glancing at her neglected cup.

A moment later, when I stood to get something out of the fridge, I instructed her to not touch my soda. But no sooner had I turned when I heard the can scrape across the counter. Without turning around I asked, "Alivia, are you drinking Daddy's soda?"

It was quiet for a moment. Then I heard the distinct sound of a can being set down and sliding back across the counter. She responded meekly, "No."

I turned around as she looked up at me, trying her hardest to seem innocent. "Alivia, are you lying to me?" I asked.

"No," she said.

Worried that I might be raising a sociopath, I pressed further. "Livvy, do you know what *lying* means?"

She looked at me as though I were crazy and said, "Yes. Lying means . . . ROAR!" As she said this last word, a ferocious look came over her, and she raised both of her little hands in the air, cupped like the paws of a lion cub.

It was so cute that disciplining her became impossible. I'm pretty sure I laughed until tears ran down my face. And I'm not sure what confused her more, my laughter or that her dad had responded to her sneaking a drink of Coke by accusing her of being a lion. To this day that is the funniest conversation I've ever had with a two-year-old and one of our favorite Lusko family memories.

SATAN: A LYING HYENA

All jokes aside, I want to warn you about a liar who also happens to be like a lion. His name is Satan. Jesus said that he is the father of lies and that there isn't a shred of truth in him (John 8:44). In other words, you can tell that the devil is lying if his lips are moving. Nothing he says can be trusted. Scripture also tells us that he "walks about like a roaring lion, seeking whom he may devour" (1 Peter 5:8). He's superdangerous too. He won't even show up except to steal, to kill, and to destroy (John 10:10). And get this: he really hates you. A lot. He's out to get you.

What's his problem? He's going to hell. God promised way back in the garden of Eden that the devil is going down. He will be crushed under our feet swiftly (Romans 16:20). There's nothing he can do about it, and he knows it. He doesn't want to go down empty-handed, though, for misery loves company. Since he can't stop God from throwing him into hell, he will try to hurt God by taking as many of the people God loves with him when he goes.

It's similar to what happens at pool parties when people get thrown into the water. They hold on to things to try to keep from being thrown in for as long as they can, but then their strategy changes when they realize it's inevitable. "If I'm going in, I'm bringing you all with me" is the prevailing thinking. That, coupled with a narcissistic god complex, just about sums up Satan's MO.

We are just pawns to the devil. He knows that we matter to God, though, and since he can't hurt God directly, he inflicts pain on him indirectly by hurting us. If you have put your faith in Jesus, Satan can't pluck you out of God's hand. More than anything, Satan wants to take you to hell, but if he can't do that, he'll try to keep you from taking anyone to heaven.

While we are no match for Satan, he is no match for God. Greater is he that is in us than he that is in the world (1 John 4:4). Satan might be *like* a lion—I think he's more of a hyena—but Jesus is *the* Lion of the tribe of Judah, the true King of the jungle. Satan would love for you to think he is all-powerful. He's not. He has to ask God for permission to mess with us. God has also established limits to temptation so that there is always a way to escape.

You can see this illustrated in the wilderness temptation of

Jesus, when Satan stood behind Jesus and told him to jump off the temple (Matthew 4:5–6). Why would the devil tell Jesus to jump? Because he couldn't push him! I guarantee that if he could have, he would have. But he could only whisper in Jesus' ear, not make him do it. So it is when Satan comes your way with his bag of tricks. He doesn't want you to know this, but he can't make you do anything. You always have a choice. In that way, you are more dangerous to yourself than the devil is. He has to check with God before he can wreak havoc in your life, but you can do great damage to your calling without getting approval from anyone.

I told you in chapter 1 that you are special, destined for impact. But know this: God's not the only one who knows you're special. Your enemy knows it, too, and he is desperate to keep you from realizing it and reaching your potential. He knows that God wants to use you to save people Satan has under his thumb, and he doesn't want it to happen. Paul said that we should not be ignorant of Satan's devices (2 Corinthians 2:11). That means we need to understand his ways and his weapons. It is absolutely vital that you pray for God to open your eyes to the invisible war being waged all around you. Seeing through the eyes of a Lion will enable you to spot the attacks of the one who comes against you like a lion. You've got to fight fire with fire.

Our biggest mistake in this war is that we often underestimate our enemy's creativity. We think he is only capable of the surprise attack, like a breaching great white shark. By default, when I think about Satan attacking, in my head I hear the *Jaws* theme song. An antagonistic coworker goes out of his way to make you look bad and lies about you for nothing other than your faith. A friend at school mocks you when she finds out you are a virgin and pressures you to get some action. Someone breaks into your house and robs you while you are on a mission trip. Outright attack is certainly an effective strategy that the devil does employ, but it is not his only trick.

SATAN'S WEAPON: BREAD AND CIRCUSES

Sticks and stones aren't the only weapons in Satan's arsenal. He often resorts to something much more dangerous, something I call *panem et circenses*. Wikipedia that if you want, but I'll save you the time—it's Latin for "bread and circuses," and it's part of a quote from a Roman writer named Juvenal from around 100 AD: "For the People who once upon a time handed out military command, high civil office, legions—everything, now restrains itself and anxiously hopes for just two things: bread and circuses."[1]

He was describing the way the people of the Roman Empire had been tricked into giving up their freedom as citizens belonging to what was once a republic. They allowed the emperors to take away their power to vote, elect their own officials, and govern themselves. These priceless things had been purchased on the cheap. All it had taken was grain and games. Food and entertainment. Bread and circuses.

During the Imperial age, under men like Julius Caesar, Augustus, Tiberius, Octavian, and Nero, as many as 135 days out of the year were dedicated to games: gladiator matches, chariot races, juggling competitions, elaborate mock naval battles, and beast hunts with exotic animals imported from far-flung provinces of the empire.[2] These emperors found that as long as people weren't hungry or bored, their freedom could be stolen. In the process, the emperors could turn themselves from kings into gods. The free food and endless entertainment acted as an anesthetic. They kept people amused while their liberty was taken. It was poison laced with sugar, and it was incredibly effective.

The leaders the people trusted were slowly subjugating them, and they loved them for it. They shortsightedly gave up things that mattered for things that were over in a short period of time. In the book *The Hunger Games* (and the movie based on it), this concept is played out in the future. The name of the capital city, Panem, is a nod to Juvenal's quote, as are the excess and indulgence depicted in the film among Panem's citizens, who feast and then vomit so they can keep eating. And though my editor will probably insist I tell you it has been debunked by historians, legend has it that at the height of the Roman Empire, among the super-rich, many decadent feasts included vomitoriums, where you could puke and then continue partying.

The devil is all over bread and circuses. It's his favorite. He wants you to give up what Christ died for you to have, and he knows that if he can distract you, he can destroy you.

That's why he doesn't always ride on his Harley like the Hells Angel that he is. Scripture says he can transform himself into an angel of light (2 Corinthians 11:14). It's not always the *Jaws* theme song he jams to—it's lighthearted, whimsical carousel music that plays while he rides in on a circus train. And let me tell you, if you think he's bad as an enemy, he's much worse and much deadlier to have as a friend. This destruction by distraction is difficult to detect when it's happening, because it doesn't involve bad things but good things that take the place of the most important things.

You must not fall for Satan's tricks. Open your eyes! Life is more than who's fighting whom on UFC, what so-and-so tweeted, which celebrities just broke up, and what the latest and greatest food truck is serving up. You were meant to live on a higher level.

> DESTRUCTION BY DISTRACTION IS DIFFICULT TO DETECT WHEN IT'S HAPPENING, BECAUSE IT DOESN'T INVOLVE BAD THINGS BUT GOOD THINGS THAT TAKE THE PLACE OF THE MOST IMPORTANT THINGS.

The devil wants to steal your power and neutralize your impact. His goal is to trick you with the trivial and get you to spend your life focused on the superficial, so that you are kept from your calling and deprived of your destiny. If he can keep your attention diverted until you are dead, he will be able to get you to do to yourself what he doesn't have the power to do to you. His endgame is to play the fiddle while the life you were meant to live goes up in smoke.

Don't mistake what I'm saying. There's nothing wrong with food or fun. Football, wine, cycling, travel, Twitter, and fashion—these are all good things God wants us to enjoy while we are on earth. I'm convinced that he takes pleasure as we enjoy our lives. Solomon said, "Go ahead. Eat your food with joy, and drink your wine with a happy heart, for God approves of this! Wear fine clothes, with a splash of cologne!" (Ecclesiastes 9:7–8 NLT). He smiles as we eat and laugh, run and play. But these things, in and of themselves, aren't enough. We were never supposed to live our lives purely on the physical playing field. We were meant for so much more.

WE DON'T BELONG HERE

In Philippians 3:19, Paul said that we are not to focus only on earthly things, for to live that way is to have your belly as your god, worshipping your body and focusing on only what you can eat, drink, and touch. Life is more than eating and the body more than what you wear (Matthew 6:25). Plus, Paul said, to live focused on things of the earth doesn't make sense for a Christian, because our citizenship is in heaven (Philippians 3:20).

Hearing this statement would have immediately fired off bells for the Philippians he was writing to. The city of Philippi was not a part of the empire—it was a Roman colony. Unlike those in neighboring cities in the region of Macedonia, those who lived in Philippi enjoyed Roman citizenship, which was a really big deal.

The majority of those in Philippi had never set foot in Rome, but they were under its protection and its privileges. In the annals of Rome their names were recorded. Though they were far from Rome, it was technically their home. They lived in Philippi, but their citizenship was somewhere else.

As a Christian, the same is true for you. You live here, but heaven is your home country. If you have put your faith in Christ, this world is no longer your home. You live in it but are not of it. You are just passing through. Your time here is just a long layover. Your current status is resident alien.

That's not just some nice thought or wishful thinking. There's a paper trail to back it up.

You see, both birth and death are citizenship-altering events. You become a citizen when you are born. The government gives you a certificate of live birth and a Social Security card, and you can get a passport, a driver's license, and so on. When you die there's paperwork too. The government sends a death certificate in the mail.

I'll never forget the day I opened up the envelope that contained Lenya's death certificate. It came exactly twenty days after she went to heaven. It was the harshest letter I've ever opened.

I was working through a stack of mail, and opening it up was like stepping on a land mine. Seeing her beautiful name on such a ghastly document was crushing. I held it in my hands and shook with sadness.

In God's grace, the next envelope I opened was from a friend, who enclosed a $50,000 check made out to our church, with Lenya's name on the memo line. His desire was for us to turn off the dark and see God make the devil pay in her honor. I felt the Lord once again calling me to channel my anger and sadness to turn the pain into seeds that could be planted and produce a harvest.

The death certificate we received that day ended my daughter's citizenship in this country. She is no longer an American. When census takers count up the total number of citizens of the United States, they don't include Abraham Lincoln. He is not a citizen anymore, either.

Salvation affects spiritual citizenship because it is an event that encompasses both birth and death. Being born again is dying: to sin, to your old life, to this world. And it's birth: new life in Christ is planted inside your chest. Just as Christ rose from the dead, you are raised to walk in newness of life. Colossians 3:3 says, "For you died, and your life is hidden with Christ in God."

Where's the paperwork for this spiritual death and birth? It was nailed to the cross. At the moment you believed, your citizenship in this world was canceled. You were transferred out of the kingdom of darkness and into the kingdom of light. And there's paperwork done for this part too. Your name is written in the Book of Life (Philippians 4:3; Luke 10:20).

From that moment on, you live in this world, but you are not *of* this world—you are a part of an entirely different kingdom.

The difficulty is that we get comfortable here so easily.

The gravitational pull of this world is constant and disorienting. Interference gets in the way of heaven's homing signal at every turn. We can be lulled into a false sense of home, but in the end, we have no choice but to leave.

CORRECTIVE LENSES

Having my daughter go to heaven in my arms acted as a cataclysmic event, opening my eyes up to eternity like never before. It shook me from my cocoon of comfort and made the bread and circuses of this world become visible and less desirable to me. In the book *Strong Fathers, Strong Daughters*, Dr. Meg Meeker described parenting as "walking around with your heart outside your chest. It goes to school and gets made fun of. It jumps into cars that go too fast. It breaks and bleeds."[3] Having my little girl leave this world made me long for the next one. It pulled my thoughts away from superficial things and took my mind behind the veil.

This is the goodness of grief, the grace of suffering. The flood of sorrow blasting its way through your soul wipes out attention previously devoted to trivial things. It's absolutely impossible to confront such powerful emotion and care about a Super Bowl commercial.

I found that grief undeniably enhanced my spiritual senses. Being so near to eternity causes you to almost be able to taste it. The unseen spiritual world becomes more vivid and more apparent than ever. There were moments, especially in the first few months after Lenya went to heaven, when I could sense the nearness of God's kingdom in a way that I had never in my life experienced. God's whisper was amplified in the deafening roar of death and loss. I suppose that is what Jesus meant by, "Blessed are those who mourn" (Matthew 5:4). There are gifts you get from God in the midst of grief that you would never have had the bandwidth to receive if everything was going as planned. It was as though a lens that had been misaligned deep inside my soul jolted into place.

When the Hubble Space Telescope first launched, hopes were high that it would return unprecedented images of outer space. The price tag was $1.5 billion, so it really needed to perform to justify the expense.[4] Unfortunately, at first it was a billion-dollar disaster. All the images that came back to earth were blurry and useless. The telescope was out of focus. The lens had been calibrated incorrectly. It was a tiny problem, a flaw in a lens only one-fiftieth the thickness of a sheet of paper, yet it caused the soaring spyglass to be nearsighted. Hubble needed glasses. It was the butt of a thousand jokes.

It was impossible to take out the damaged lens and far too expensive to bring Hubble home for repairs, so scientists and engineers devised a brilliant solution. They would effectively put a giant contact lens on the telescope. They built an additional optical component with the exact same error—but inverted—and added it to the telescope. Bingo! All of a sudden Hubble could see like a supersonic eagle. It had twenty-twenty vision on steroids. Never in the history of the world have we seen more glorious pictures or had such knowledge of the universe as what Hubble has beamed back to our dark planet.[5]

That was what Lenya's homecoming did to our hearts. Just as her corneas gave two people physical sight, her being violently pulled from our lives and called to the distant shore of heaven snapped a "Lenya lens" into place, opening up our vision to see what we couldn't see before. As the old hymn puts it, the things of this world grew strangely dim in the light of his glory and grace.[6] While I can enjoy this world, I don't want it. I want something far greater. My soul cries out for what my daughter is experiencing. I long for the hidden treasures and secret pleasures that are in store for me in the presence of Jesus. There is still work to be done here, but deep down I can't wait for Jennie, Alivia, Daisy, Clover, and me to all finish our races and go home.

I have heard that author and speaker Joni Erickson Tada describes her paralysis as the best thing that ever happened to her and her wheelchair as a gift of grace. I understand exactly what she means and am so thankful for the gift of spiritual sight suffering has produced in my life. The very notion of appreciating anything about what you are going through right now might seem absolutely incomprehensible, especially if you are in the early and traumatic days of dealing with the ending of your parents' marriage, mourning the loss of a career, or coming out of shock into the depths of sorrow upon sorrow. But I believe the day will come when you will see that God always grants incredible power to those called to face impossible pain.

I SEEK A HOMELAND

Fortunately, great loss is not the only way to combat the bread and circuses that Satan uses to trip you up. Nor is it a silver bullet that makes you immune for the rest of your life; the further you get from the ground zero of your loss, the more its effects fade with time. We must learn to be diligent at thinking differently. Paul told us to *set* our mind on things above. You must make an active, ongoing decision to walk in faith.

To see this decision in action, look at Abraham, the father of faith:

> By faith Abraham obeyed when he was called to go out . . . And he went out, not knowing where he was going. By faith he dwelt in the land of promise as in a foreign country, dwelling in tents with Isaac and Jacob, the heirs with him of the same promise; for he waited for the city which has foundations, whose builder and maker is God. (Hebrews 11:8–10)

There are so many Old Testament saints—regular peeps like Abel, Noah, Esther, David, and Daniel—who did the same. Listen to what the New Testament TiVo account says when you rewind the first half of the Bible and play it back without the commercials:

> These all died in faith, not having received the promises, but having seen them afar off were assured of them, embraced them and confessed that they were strangers and pilgrims on the earth. For those who say such things declare plainly that they seek a homeland. (Hebrews 11:13–14)

We must face up and then fess up to the fact that we are pilgrims. We need to tell ourselves that we are strangers and aliens and plainly declare that our home country is heaven.

My wife put a sign on the wall on her side of our bedroom that says, "I seek a homeland." It is the first thing she sees when she sits up to get out of bed. She wants putting this perspective on to be part of her daily routine, just like getting dressed and brushing her teeth. It's a daily choice, not a one-time thing.

The more passionate you are about setting your soul to

heaven's time zone, the more progress you will make in your calling here on earth. There is no greater aid to holy living than living in light of the glory that is to come when Christ returns, or when we die and stand before him. 1 John 3:3 says, "Everyone who has this hope in Him purifies himself, just as He is pure." Thinking of what you want to be found doing during Christ's return is an incredible motivator. Focus on it often.

> THE MORE PASSIONATE YOU ARE ABOUT SETTING YOUR SOUL TO HEAVEN'S TIME ZONE, THE MORE PROGRESS YOU WILL MAKE IN YOUR CALLING HERE ON EARTH.

The secret is to view yourself as a pilgrim just passing through. Like John Bunyan's Christian, you are on your way to the Celestial City, the capital of Christ's kingdom that can't be shaken.

The progress a traveler makes is driven by his passion for the destination. The more you talk and think about what it will be like when Jesus returns, the more fearless you will become as you go face Apollyon's arrows or go through Vanity Fair, the slough of Despond, or the Valley of the Shadow of Death. The more you will desire to store up treasure in heaven and reach out to others on the way. It is through constantly setting our minds on things above that we will be able to see through the temptations of the trivial here below and set aside the weights that hinder us from running our races with joy.

Pastor Greg Laurie and his wife, Cathe, are so good at texting Jennie and me little verses and encouragements, often exactly when we need them. More than once I have known the Holy Spirit triggered them to send an encouragement during a low moment. One day they sent us this quote from E. M. Bounds that perfectly sums up the power we can have over the temptation of bread and circuses:

> Heaven ought to draw and engage us. Heaven ought to so fill our hearts and hands, our manner, and our conversation, our character and our features, that all would see that we are foreigners, strangers to this world. . . . The very atmosphere of the world should be chilling to us and noxious, its suns eclipsed and its companionship dull and insipid. Heaven is our native land and home to us, and death to us is not the dying hour, but the birth hour.[7]

THE HARM OF BEING HYBRID

In the 1990s a breeding experiment between Asiatic and African lions in India went horribly wrong. Scientists tried to mix the two together, but it backfired. The hybrid lions' back legs were too weak to support them. Some were so feeble they couldn't even eat meat off the bone and had to be served boneless meat.

There were originally about eighty of these hybrids, a figure that was down to twenty-one when I read about it.[8] They are kept in a small enclosure, nicknamed the "old age home" for lions. Those who take care of them are basically just waiting for them to die. The photos of these pitiful creatures were heartbreaking. One reporter noted that the lions "are extremely weak. They can barely stand up or walk. Their only activity is a small but painful walk to eat their meals. However, if challenged, they can still muster a spine-chilling roar."[9]

This sad story is a picture of what is at stake if you don't fight to keep your heart set on heaven. The enemy wants to clip your wings and declaw your calling. If he can get you to mix enough compromise into your life, he will slowly be able to slip a muzzle over your snout. You are meant to live a life that's not laced, totally offered up to God as a living sacrifice. Too many Christians are tricked out of their power through their purity being diluted and their perspective being grounded. Refuse to live a life that is "cut." Don't hobble back and forth between Jesus and the world, or slowly you will become like a sickly hybrid version of the "you" you were born to be.

Keep your eyes on the true Lion, and you'll see through the lies of the enemy.

ELEVEN

RUN TOWARD THE ROAR

Jennie and I were lying next to Daisy and Alivia in their beds, talking about how close we were to one year of Lenya being in heaven.

"Wait, how many days will that be?" Alivia asked.

"Three hundred and sixty-five days," I said.

She looked surprised and sighed deeply.

I asked, "How many days does it feel like it's been to you?"

She thought about it for a moment and said, "Sometimes it feels like it's only been two days, and sometimes it feels like it's been a thousand."

Truer words were never spoken. There is a disorienting endlessness to suffering that makes it easy to lose your bearings. It's like being lost in the woods of your own soul. Initially, just surviving each moment without hyperventilating is so all-consuming that minutes tick by slower than years. But then one day you poke your head out from your hibernation of hurting, and it can be shocking to find that actual time has passed.

The first year is gnarly. Every ten feet there is a land mine waiting to detonate. The moment you lose someone, holidays instantly go from happy to hard. Mother's and Father's Days, Easter, the Fourth of July—these are all times when the absence of someone you love is exaggerated. In moments when you would always be together or in times when you had special traditions, the ache gets a little bit louder. The first time the person's birthday comes around, it will be unspeakably difficult. A birthday is an awkward, clumsy thing when you can't be with the person whose day you so badly long to celebrate.

Not too long after Lenya went to heaven, it hit me how profoundly different the Christmas season would be for us for the rest of our lives. It would be impossible for us to ever experience the merriest time of the year without triggering traumatic and horrifying memories. Unfortunately for us, the retail juggernaut that is Christmas in America has stretched out its tentacles so wide and far that in some stores you begin to see decorations before the leaves have even started falling off the trees. This all-important time for businesses to get in the black necessitates them pumping gingerbread and holly into the air so aggressively that the holidays approach with the subtlety and restraint of a runaway freight train.

By the time we reached our first Halloween without Lenya, I was thinking about how Thanksgiving was all that separated us from the anniversary of her departure and the bevy of difficult days that would come along with it: Christmas Eve, Christmas Day, and the anniversary of her funeral, which took place the morning after Christmas. There would be no hiding from any of it, not if we planned on staying in America, anyway. Everything about our nation shifts into a giant countdown. Little numbered doors hiding chocolate. Eleven lords-a-leaping, five golden eggs, and a partridge in a pear tree.

It hit me—I was actually scared of Christmas. My gut reaction was to run, to get away from it all. We could pull a John Grisham and just skip it.

THE NEAREST LION MAY BE BEHIND YOU

I am fascinated by the way lions hunt. I've read that it's the lionesses that actually do the "lion's share" of the work. The males are obviously incredibly intimidating, with their manes and their ferocious roars, but it's the chicks you really have to watch out for.

The fact that lionesses do not have a big, recognizable mane actually helps them sneak up on whatever they are hunting. They lie in wait, hidden in the tall grass, motionless like statues. I listened to a sermon by Pastor Brian Houston in which he said that the males do play an important, albeit small, role. While the females stalk their prey from behind, the king of the jungle will come from the front and let loose one of those roars that gives him his spot at the top of the food chain. This sound is so powerful it can be heard for up to five miles away. Hearing that terrifying noise causes the gazelle or antelope to run as far as they can away from whatever made that sound.

What they don't know is that as scary as it sounded, the one who did the roaring is more bark than bite. So away they go—directly into the path of the real threat: the waiting lioness. In other words, the prey's instincts are wrong. Going with their guts causes them to make the last mistake of their short, little lives. It's counterintuitive, but the right choice would be to override their emotions and run *toward* the roar.

It's shocking how often that is true. When you run from things that scare you, you move toward danger, not away from it. If you fail to face your fears, they will always be right there behind you. You must suppress the little voice inside that's telling you to get out of Dodge. It is not your friend. When you feel that panicky fight-or-flight sensation and you want to run away, do the opposite. Run toward the roar. You have come into the kingdom for just such a time as this (Esther 4:14).

Jennie and I made this decision as we chose how we were going to respond to the terrible nightmare of having our daughter taken from us. Everyone grieves differently. It's a process, not a science. But we decided that we would go through it running toward the roar. Here is an excerpt from my journal, where I described our approach.

> We grieved staring this thing in the face. When unpacking the bag [Lenya] had brought to her grandma's containing the clothes she had worn that Thursday, before changing into her pj's that she died in, it was extremely tempting to hide from it or cling to it. Either keeping them as keepsakes, making all her clothing sacred, or not opening it at all, refusing to go there. But we chose to hug them and weep over them, smelling her on them, and then we washed them so they would be folded and in the drawer for Daisy and then Clover to wear one day. Nothing would be sacred. We didn't want boxes full of mementos waiting to blow us up when we stepped on them in ten years. Looking at pictures, watching movies,

going through her clothes—we made the choice to bring this thing to our breast and let it sink its teeth into us and empty its venom. For some reason, though it terrified me, I had to stare this in the eyes and, with my knees shaking, say, "Do your worst." Maybe it will kill us, but if we can get through it we won't have to live in fear. I didn't want anything sneaking up on me. I would go all the way into the depths of this sorrow and drink it down to the dregs. I stayed up til 3:00 a.m. or later each night for four or five days, watching videos, pulling out photos, and reliving her five years on this earth, to find all the best clips and pictures to play at her celebration so the world would know who she was. It was horrendously traumatic and would have been easier to take a Xanax and stay in bed crying . . . but I knew it would only delay the inevitable. No shrines, no booby traps . . . we faced it all, and then pushed on into the future.

One of the most difficult days was when the hospital gave us a box with the things Lenya had been wearing in the emergency room. I didn't want to open it. We felt like running in the opposite direction. But eventually Jennie and I braced ourselves and faced it. The box contained her little socks, leggings, and the top that had been cut off her with medical scissors. All the emergency room personnel had written on a card they included in the package. At the bottom was an ink handprint and footprint an ER nurse had thoughtfully captured from Lenya's hands and feet as a keepsake.

Jennie and I wept on the floor as we pulled these items out, one by one. It felt as if fire were burning underneath my skin, and my brain grew hot. The socks, more than anything, destroyed me. It was more than I could bear. We cried together and called on the Lord and prayed for the people who worked in the ER. And then we got up.

I pray you never have to have your heart pierced with a sword like that, but like it or not, in ways small and large, we are all going to have to confront our fears or abandon our destinies. The only path to the haul of fish you are meant to catch and the lives you are meant to reach is to launch out into the deep and sail through things that are scary. Smooth seas never made a skilled sailor. God calls us to go to places that frighten us so that we will fully trust him. The only way for you to see God do the kinds of things he desires to do in and through you is to run toward the roar again and again and again.

> THE ONLY WAY FOR YOU TO SEE GOD DO THE KINDS OF THINGS HE DESIRES TO DO IN AND THROUGH YOU IS TO RUN TOWARD THE ROAR AGAIN AND AGAIN AND AGAIN.

I see this tenacity of spirit in the life of young David. When he confronted Goliath in the valley of Elah, he didn't walk to face the nine-foot warrior who was spewing out death threats against the young shepherd. He *ran*: "So it was, when the Philistine arose and came and drew near to meet David, that David hurried and ran toward the army to meet the Philistine" (1 Samuel 17:48). It's incredible that David was willing to fight Goliath at all. The fact that he sprinted toward what seemed like certain death is astounding. He killed the giant in the end, but first he had to run toward the very thing that terrified him the most.

What in your life are you being called to right now? Perhaps it's a song you are meant to write or a church you are meant to plant. Maybe it's pulling your children out of school to educate them at home or allowing your son to go to a public school so he can share his faith and be salt and light. Are you vacillating between the safety of a job you hate and the terrifying prospect of starting your own business? Maybe you are supposed to go back to school, or on the other hand, it might be that you should opt out of college in order to pursue a different kind of education.

I can't tell you what God's will for your life is. As I said before, there is no magic map. All I can tell you is that you must not let fear play a part in your decision making. You can't ignore fear, but you don't have to let it control you. I guarantee you David's pulse thundered like a war drum in his chest, and everything in him urged him to retreat, but he still hustled toward the giant. True bravery isn't feeling no fear—it's being afraid and moving forward anyway.

I know this for sure: Turning your back on the roar will feel good in the moment. You will feel a euphoric giddiness once you have put some distance between yourself and the lunacy you were considering. *Cooler heads prevailed*, you will think as you wipe the dust off your hands and prepare to return to business as usual. But hiding in the thicket, far from the sound of the wild calling you are meant to pursue, is a far more sinister opponent you didn't even know was there: death. The death of the dreams God planted deep down inside you. The death of the life you were born to live. Like a slow leak in your tire that saps your ability to drive your car, you will have robbed yourself of the opportunity to stare down something that scared you. Live this way long enough, and the muscles of your faith will eventually atrophy. To quote the immortal William Wallace from the movie *Braveheart*,

> Aye, fight and you may die. Run, and you'll live . . . at least a while. And dying in your beds, many years from now, would

> you be willin' to trade *all* the days, from this day to that, for one chance, just one chance, to come back here and tell our enemies that they may take our lives, but they'll never take . . . *our freedom*![1]

Yes, running toward the roar can be excruciating, and there are no guarantees. It's also possible to misjudge the direction of the roar you are trying to run toward. It could be a dead end. When you live a life of faith, there are going to be questions that have no answers, because for there to be faith, there has to be mystery. That's just life in the deep end. It would be nice if we could have the safety of the shore and the potential of the open ocean at the same time, but that's not how it works. Nothing ventured, nothing gained. If you want to catch fish you have to launch out where the fish live.

LET IT (THE FEAR OF FAILURE) GO

Often what keeps us in the shallows is our fear of failure. Know this: not only is failure not a bad thing—it is a necessary thing. The only way to get to victory is to be willing to make mistakes on the way there. True overnight successes are rare. Far more often, you must keep showing up, day in and day out, until the hard, unglamorous work adds up and pays off. It's easy to misunderstand what you are seeing when you look at people taking a victory lap or receiving attention or promotion. Their celebration is only the tip of the iceberg. Invisible to your eye is what's underwater—the hell they went through on the road to success.

I recently read a powerful story about Kristen Anderson-

Lopez. She, along with her husband, Robert, wrote the song "Let It Go" from Disney's *Frozen*. Like many of you, my family and I have not only seen this film a hundred times, but we own the soundtrack as well. (And no, I would *not* like to build a snowman.) "Let It Go" is not just a great song—it is literally the best. It won an Oscar for the best song in a motion picture in 2013. It's so good that it changed the course of the movie: Apparently Elsa, the character in the movie who freezes everything, was originally going to stay bad. The slot where "Let It Go" fits into the movie was going to have a liberated and evil Elsa singing a song that was dubbed in the story outline as "Elsa's Badass Song." But when the directors heard "Let It Go" they were so moved that they rewrote everything so Elsa could be redeemed.

Kristen also wrote seventeen songs that weren't included in the movie. *Seventeen* times her songs weren't right. *Seventeen* times she heard "no." Most of us would consider ourselves colossal failures if we were shut down five or six times. It would be difficult to keep pressing full steam ahead after being rejected a dozen times. But she continued writing and creating and inventing and putting herself out there *seventeen* times.

Let that sink in. Songs #1, 2, 3, 4, 5, 6, 7, 8, 9, 10, 11, 12, 13, 14, 15, 16, and 17 weren't good enough for the movie. Attempt number 18 was a different story. This time the movie, as it was currently written, wasn't good enough for the song.[2]

The point is that to envy someone's success is to completely misunderstand the nature of it. To covet the limelight and the accolades is to focus on the wrong thing. Yes, there are those who are given every advantage and people who are raised with silver spoons in their mouths, but far more often the recipe for success is simple and unpleasant. You persevere through difficulty, bad ideas, bad days, and bitterness again and again and again, until something clicks. It's not sexy, but it's true. What you are willing to do in secret is so often responsible for what happens in public. It would be nice to crank out a hit on your first attempt, but those unlucky enough to do so often end up unable to replicate their accidental success. Far better to be okay with writing some duds and, as the plucky Dory says in *Finding Nemo*, "just keep swimming."

A MANIFESTO IN THE FACE OF FEAR

Perhaps for you running toward the roar isn't about something you're supposed to do but rather something difficult you have to go through: painful chemotherapy treatments, a divorce, a move across the country that will dislocate you from friendships that mean the world to you. Sometimes there is no other alternative but to face it.

People often tell me, "I don't know how you've managed to survive. I don't think I could do it if I were you." When I hear that kind of thing, the response in my head is often, *I don't think I can make it through this, either!* But what choice have I had? No one gave me an option. I didn't sign up for this.

When you have no alternative but to endure something you are afraid of, you can still exhibit bravery. It has everything to do with your attitude and outlook. Christmas is going to arrive each year, whether I like it or not. Santa Claus is, in fact, going to come to town, and there's nothing I can do to stop it. My choice is whether I will merely hunker down and try to survive the holidays and the painful associations that come with them, or harness my pain and, in the midst of the turmoil, try to shine the light and turn off the dark for as many people as possible—and myself in the process. I'd rather run toward Christmas than hide from it.

Remember this: God isn't scared of what you're scared of. But you don't have to pretend like you're not frightened. Naming your fear is part of getting through it. It's also important to remember that Immanuel means "God with us." Jesus is with you. You are never alone. Whisper to him, "I know you're here" when you find yourself trembling and wanting to bolt.

GOD ISN'T SCARED OF WHAT YOU'RE SCARED OF.

Here's a little manifesto I wrote regarding Christmas and the Lusko family. I encourage you to borrow the idea next time you are scared.

> We will celebrate the birth of the One who came to destroy death and bring light and immortality to light through the gospel. We will sing until our voices won't let us. We will preach and celebrate seeing people come to know Jesus, just as we did days after Lenya died in my arms. We will party if we can muster the courage, cry when we miss her, and collapse if we have to. Even though he slays us, we will bless his name. We always have a choice, and we choose to rejoice.

God has been with me through the flashbacks, the sleepless nights, the tears, and the lack of tears. He has been with me when I feel so condemned for my mistakes as Lenya's dad that I want to hurt myself. I missed her last ballet open class (one parents were allowed to attend) because of a meeting at work, and thinking about it takes my breath away. I second-guess myself for the times I lost my temper, or when I was too busy or distracted by technology to be in a moment I can never get back. There are judgment calls I made in the moment that I obsess over but can't do anything about. Looking back, I feel like such a failure. I have found myself paralyzed by regret and wanting to become a crazy, old recluse, replaying my blooper reel and muttering, "Laces out, Marino!"[3] But each time Jesus has been with me and given me the strength to face my fears. He will do the same for you.

FACING UP TO MR. FREEZE

One summer we took a family trip to Six Flags Over Texas. I recently came across a picture from that day and asked Alivia what her favorite ride was. Without thinking about it, she said, "Mr. Freeze."

Her answer surprised me. She had been *terrified* of that ride. I have never seen such fear in her eyes. For some reason she got spooked at the last minute, just as our turn came to board. I tried to reason with her. She had already ridden all the other scary, upside-down, g-force-inducing rides in the park. Mr. Freeze is a ride based on a bad guy played by Arnold Schwarzenegger in the lamest Batman movie ever made; come on, how scary could it be? I rattled off three rides we had gone on that were worse than Mr. Freeze, but it didn't help. Fear is irrational. When I saw tears in her eyes, we bailed through the emergency exit.

Later in the day, she announced she was ready. To be honest, I wasn't completely sure she would go through with it, but she clenched her teeth, sat down, and buckled up. Blastoff! When the ride ended, Alivia had this jubilant look in her eyes that you can only get by prying joy from the clenched fist of fear. I think it is telling that in the rearview mirror, the memory that stuck with her was not the ride with the most vertical feet but the one where she won a victory over herself. Facing her fears, she had run toward the roar, and she loved it.

Some superwise person once observed that most people die at twenty-five and aren't buried until they're seventy-five. Don't let that happen to you. Don't let your soul stop growing, and don't give in even if your stomach is growling. Your greatest days are still to come. I dare you to believe that the day will come where what you are most scared of right now will be included in your highlight reel as a triumphant victory. The only way to truly live is to run toward the roar.

TWELVE

PENCILS DOWN

I can't think of any two words I associate with a terrible feeling in the pit of my stomach more than the phrase, "Pencils down." It is the sound of a hundred tests I wasn't prepared for.

I have never tested well. I especially hated all the timed, standardized tests with those little bubbles. I don't know what it was exactly—the pressure, the way the rooms were so quiet . . . or the fact that I never studied. Taking tests was never my sweet spot, that's for sure.

There would always be that one student who would finish seemingly within moments of the test starting. And every single time, *that* guy would always walk as loudly as he could to the teacher's desk to turn in his work, and then he would turn and look at the class smugly before taking his seat as though to say, "Totally nailed it. And maybe if you would have worked harder, you could have too."

The worst part, of course, is how the teacher would look at the clock on the wall and pronounce the test over by saying, "All right, everybody. Time's up—pencils down!" I don't know what you did when teachers said that, but I know what I did—I tore through the remaining questions, filling in as many bubbles as I could: C, C, C, C, C, C, C, C . . . I figured that one out of four was better odds than zero out of four!

"I said, 'Pencils down,' Levi!" my teacher would chide.

I'd suggest that someone ought to track down my sixth grade English teacher and let her know I wrote a book, except I'd genuinely be afraid that Mrs. Barajas would be so shocked she would drop dead on the spot.

That is actually what I want to leave you with in this final chapter—not Mrs. Barajas dropping dead, but the inevitability of you dropping dead.

Okay, yeah, I know what you're probably thinking: *Hey, Lusko, way to end on a low note! Lighten up, dude, and put your feet on the sunny side of the street!*

Honestly, that's exactly what I'm doing. There's something really awesome I have to tell you. Just hang with me for a minute.

Here's the truth of it: life is a timed test. We're all living against a deadline. The Bible tells us that a moment is coming when God will say, "Pencils down" to each one of us: "It is appointed for men to die once, but after this the judgment" (Hebrews 9:27).

Deadline is a word we use to describe the time when a project or an application is due. You might be surprised to know that the origin of that word actually has something to do with real dying. In the early 1900s, it was a physical line painted on the ground around the inside of a prison, measured out twenty feet from the walls. If prisoners crossed this line, they would be shot on the spot.[1] It was literally a line of death.

But really, that's how life is. At a certain point we cross a line, and it's all over. But none of us know where that deadline is. It's invisible. Sand keeps falling from our hourglasses, but there is no way to know how much we started with or how much we have left. We may have an appointment with death, but it's not on our Google calendars.

WE MAY HAVE AN APPOINTMENT WITH DEATH, BUT IT'S NOT ON OUR GOOGLE CALENDARS.

James, the brother of Jesus, pointed this fact out when he said, "Come now, you who say, 'Today or tomorrow we will go to such and such a city, spend a year there, buy and sell, and make a profit'; whereas you do not know what will happen tomorrow. For what is your life? It is even a vapor that appears for a little time and then vanishes away" (James 4:13–14).

You only get so much time to live, and then—ready or not—it's over. One of the only truly certain things about life is that it will end. Far better than living in denial about the fact that our lives will end is facing up to it and living in light of it. The only people who are truly ready to live are those who are prepared to die.

PREMONITIONS

One of my favorite preachers is a man from Scotland named Robert Murray McCheyne. He lived during the 1800s and was an amazing man of God. His sermons and journal entries are incredible. When I was starting out in ministry at the ripe age of nineteen, I read a biography about him that said he had weak lungs and died before he turned thirty.[2]

When I read that biography, I thought, *That is going to be me.* Between the suicidal thoughts I had when I was young and the asthma that would occasionally land me in the hospital, I had always thought I would die young. It's twisted, I know, but somehow the thought encouraged me. McCheyne was a bright light for God, and though he only lived a short time on the earth, he accomplished much. I made it my aim to channel all my energy and passion into each moment, and I have always sought to preach every message as though it were my last. The assumption that I didn't have much time on the clock made me not want to waste a second.

As my twenties went on, and I got married and began a family, I thought less and less about dying young. The thought of going out in a blaze of glory in the pulpit is much less appealing as a father of four children who need a dad than it is when you are twenty, single, and carefree. By the time I was in my thirties, the thought was all but completely out of my head.

Strangely enough, in the days leading up to Lenya going to heaven, I began to think about my mortality a lot. Jennie and I were on a flight to the East Coast, and I was reading Bill O'Reilly's *Killing Kennedy*, which had just come out. It was the same trip when we would see *Spider-Man: Turn Off the Dark*. I know that for my parents' generation, the assassination of Kennedy was a defining moment. I think for millennials, the equivalent is 9/11. My dad can remember exactly where he was when JFK was killed. I have grown up knowing of President Kennedy's death as historical fact, but with no emotion or larger significance.

Reading this book caused me to be hit with the anguish of Kennedy's death in a major way. I got swept up in the story and was dreading the ending. (The downside of reading a biography is the knowledge of how it will turn out.) I kept telling Jennie she needed to read the book, and I specifically remember telling her about the crazy fact that Billy Graham had called President

Kennedy just a week before Kennedy was assassinated in Texas and warned him not to go to Dallas. Billy had a terrible feeling about the visit and didn't want the president to take the trip for fear that something awful would happen. He went anyway, and the quick trip to Dallas turned out to be his last on this earth.

This made me think about how President Lincoln, in the weeks leading up to his death, would have dreams in which he was dead. He would try to talk to his wife, Mary, about them, but they would upset her. Eventually he just kept his dreams to himself, and he lived under the dark shadow of feeling as if his death were approaching. Like Kennedy, he was assassinated, dying on Good Friday—the same day Jesus, who also constantly referred to his impending death, died.

Once again, I began to have nagging thoughts that I was going to die soon. The final few days before Lenya went home, death was everywhere. The Sandy Hook shooting was all over the news. My friend Robert, who pastors a church in Arizona, had his wife suddenly go home to heaven after a battle with cancer. A radio talk-show host in Los Angeles I had worked with over the years, who had been in a coma after a motorcycle accident, went to heaven. In the last picture I have with Lenya, I am wearing a black suit, because I had just returned home from doing a funeral for a vibrant teenage girl here in Montana who had been cut down in the prime of life. So much death.

At 4:59 p.m. on December 17, 2012, overwhelmed by all that I was feeling and needing to vent, I sent a text message to my dad: "I have been having premonitions of my death all day." He responded, and then I added, "But I have been having those since I was a child." I didn't know that, as I sent that message, we had only three days left with our Lenya Lion on this earth. It would not be Levi Aaron Lusko who would be shuffling off this mortal coil, but my daughter who, more than all her sisters, looked most like me, Lenya Avery Lusko. Looking back, I suppose in God's grace I was being prepared for our confrontation with eternity. Whether you are having premonitions of death or not, life really is a vapor (James 4:14), and every day we are only a step away from the grave (1 Samuel 20:3).

This is true for us, those we love, and those we are meant to impact. Job said, "My time is short—what's left of my life races off too fast for me to even glimpse the good. My life is going fast, like a ship under full sail, like an eagle plummeting to its prey" (Job 9:25–26 THE MESSAGE). We must live each day all the way to the hilt, because each day could be our final one here. Death could show up at any time, and it often doesn't call ahead.

Before Lenya went to be with Jesus, when I thought of death, I would focus more on leaving earth than on going to heaven. But what I have become aware of is that death is not just a departure—it is also an arrival. I used to somewhat fatalistically think about my exit, but now more than ever, I am focused on my entrance.

There is a poem called "The Two Ships," by Francis Bret Harte, which frames this idea perfectly:

As I stand by the cross on the lone mountain's crest,
Looking over the ultimate sea,
In the gloom of the mountain a ship lies at rest,
And one sails away from the lea:
One spreads its white wings on a far-reaching track,
With pennant and sheet flowing free;
One hides in the shadow with sails laid aback,—
The ship that is waiting for me!

But lo, in the distance the clouds break away!
The Gate's glowing portals I see;
And I hear from the outgoing ship in the bay
The song of the sailors in glee:
So I think of the luminous footprints that bore
The comfort o'er dark Galilee,
And wait for the signal to go to the shore
To the ship that is waiting for me.[3]

Did you catch all that? One ship is out on the open ocean, blasting toward its destination at full mast. That one carries my daughter Lenya, bound for the distant shores of heaven. The ship waiting in the darkness down at the dock is the boat I will board one day soon. It is waiting for me. Jesus will call my name, and I will embark on my journey, following in my Savior's and my daughter's footsteps, making my way home.

PLUS ULTRA AND CARPE DIEM

So here it is, the game-changing perspective: it's so much better to look forward to eternal life than it is to live fearing death.

I have incorporated a Latin phrase into a tattoo of a ship on the inside of my right arm. It says *Plus Ultra*, which means "more beyond." In the days before the new world was discovered, the official motto of Spain was *Ne Plus Ultra*, or "Nothing more beyond." The Spaniards believed that the Strait of Gibraltar was the end of the earth and that they had already explored as far as you can go. Once Columbus sailed the ocean blue, the *Ne* disappeared, and to this day on the Spanish coin is the humble acknowledgment that there is in fact more beyond.[4]

The phrase is a reminder to me that this life is not all there is. There is a hereafter. When we leave this world, we get to go home. And the way we live here has a direct impact on what we experience when we arrive there.

I began this book by telling you that you are destined for impact. There is greatness inside of you. Unlimited potential. A holy calling on your life that would make you tremble if you could fully understand. In chapter 8, I warned you that there is a price you will have to pay to activate your calling, and in chapter 10 I showed you that the devil will do anything he can to keep you from hitting your full stride. I want to leave you with a vital word of warning: potential is perishable.

Potential has a short shelf life, an expiration date that is approaching. Your calling isn't a Twinkie. Like milk or produce, it won't keep forever. It can spoil and go bad. These works God wants to do in your life? If you don't seize them, they can pass you by. You have a limited amount of time to act on the plans God has for your life before they are out of reach.

This is a timed test. There is a deadline. God is going to say, "Pencils down." And anything you don't tap into by the time this life ends shall remain undone forever.

> THIS IS A TIMED TEST. THERE IS A DEADLINE. GOD IS GOING TO SAY, "PENCILS DOWN."

This is why Jesus said in John 9:4, "I must work . . . while it is day; the night is coming when no one can work." As the well-worn adage goes, "Only one life, 'twill soon be past, only what's done for Christ will last."[5] There are things you can do on earth that will be impossible one minute after you die. Bringing comfort to the discouraged, feeding the hungry, sharing the gospel—these are all things that will be impossible to do in heaven but we can do right now.

I heard of a winning lottery ticket that was never cashed in. It was worth $77 million! The winner got the hard part right by picking the correct numbers, but for whatever reason the person never picked up the winnings. The deadline came and went. At midnight, that paper went from being worth millions of dollars to being a gum wrapper. All because the winner never rose up and laid claim to what was theirs.

My prayer is that you won't let that be your story. You have been given a powerful calling in Christ, great and mighty works he wants you to walk in. God is for you, not against you. He has planted dreams in your heart and protection around your life. You are both loved and unstoppable in the will of God. But what you do with all that is up to you. Your calling must be activated. You must make the choice to walk by faith and see what can't be seen with the naked eye. You must rise up and lay claim to what is yours in Christ Jesus our Lord. Anything that hasn't been seized by the time you die is instantly forfeited.

Before we know it, we will be standing before God to receive our reward. This tent is dissolving. It is fragile, vulnerable, and temporary, and it will soon come down. You have no way of knowing when it will end.

My daughter's life ended the night *before* the world was supposedly going to end. There was all that hoopla about the Mayan calendar and how December 21, 2012, would be the earth's last day. But they were wrong. The world is still spinning, but Lenya is not on it anymore. People talk a lot about the end of the world, but the end of your life might come first.

Night is coming—for you and for me. Getting to heaven has nothing to do with our righteous works. Our entrance fee is paid for fully by Jesus and his perfect sacrifice. But Scripture is clear that our treasure in heaven is connected to our lives on earth. It is possible to go into eternity with a saved soul and a wasted life. The missionary Amy Carmichael said, "We will have all of eternity to celebrate the victories, and only a few hours before sunset in which to win them."[6] This fact should motivate us, as it motivated Paul, who said, "Whether I live today or die—I only want to please Him" (Philippians 1:20, author's paraphrase).

The devil will do anything he can to keep you from sensing the urgency that will mark your life if you wake up each day knowing it could be your last. He won't try to talk you out of doing the things you are intended to; he'll simply tell you to put it off. One of his biggest lies is, "You can do it tomorrow." He knows what you need to know—there might not be a tomorrow. Today could be your one and only chance to be kind to that stranger, tell your kids about Jesus, or invite that person to church. You need to carpe the heck out of this diem!

Make no mistake: God will accomplish all he wants to do. The question is, will you let him do it through you? As Mordecai told Esther in Esther 4:14, if you don't rise up, help will arise from another place.

That's why Jesus was born in a cave, not a hotel. The baby was coming no matter what, and no one could stop God's plan. It's fascinating to me to think the opportunity to be the birthplace of the Messiah was offered to the hotel first. That inn could have been put on the map. How would that have been for Yelp? "Uh . . . so, our rooms are spacious . . . and did we mention . . . God was born here? But he wasn't born there, because there was no room available for him."

It's the same with you and me: if we won't stand up and do what God has planned for us, he will bless the person down the block or the church around the corner with the opportunity. Whenever his still small voice calls us to do something, it's as though we are given the right of first refusal. Warren Weirsbe, the author of the profound book *On Being a Servant of God*, once said, "It's not ability God is looking for but availability." Too often we are full of ourselves; God can use us only when we offer him our emptiness.

A thousand years from now, we won't be able to change what we did in our lifetimes, but if we do it right, we will be enjoying the fruits from it. To quote the words of Maximus from *Gladiator*—quite possibly the best movie ever made—"What we do in life echoes in eternity."[7] I pray that no matter what life throws your way, you would honor God, give him space to move in your life, and run toward the roar with all your heart until you stand before him face-to-face.

Afterword

TO INFINITY AND BEYOND

One day while I was studying, my two oldest daughters came into my office and wanted to hang out with me. I decided to involve them in what I was doing. I thought I would teach them how to write a sermon that they could then take turns preaching.

Alivia and Lenya each picked a verse to speak on and looked it up in their Bibles. I gave them some paper from a legal pad, and I told them to title their messages and write down the text and anything else they wanted to say about it. Alivia's was pretty elaborate, with subpoints and a pretty lengthy exposition (for a seven-year-old, anyway). Lenya's was far more concise.

The title of her message was "I Love God," which she had written at the top of the page. Below that was a simplified version of her verse, Mark 12:30: "Love God with all your heart." And then she filled the rest of the page up with squiggles and drawings.

I found it in my office several months after she went to heaven. Reading it felt as if she were speaking directly to me and giving me my marching orders all at the same time. "I love God, Dad," I could hear her saying. "Love him with all your heart."

The one and only sermon of Lenya Lion.

The wisest man who ever lived said that words fitly spoken are like apples of gold in settings of silver (Proverbs 25:11). If I had a hundred thousand words to work with, I could never write a message more powerful than what she wrote down that day.

On the night she went to heaven, I did for Lenya what a daddy should never have to do. I reached out and closed my little girl's eyes. What I never expected was that God would use her to open mine.

ACKNOWLEDGMENTS

I wrote "publish or perish" as my New Year's resolution at the beginning of 2012 and was working on a different book as the year came to a close. Once Lenya went home, the fire for that project went out, and I spent 2013 distilling the raw materials that would eventually be fashioned into *Through the Eyes of a Lion*. It flowed hot and turbulent, mostly into my iPhone, in a note file that soon bulged with lessons and reflections that I knew deep down would one day find their home inside the pages of a book. Over Bang-Bang Shrimp with Steven Furtick (my spiritual big brother whom, along with his wife, Holly, I am so thankful for), God confirmed the time had come for me to open the floodgates and let the lion out of the cage. I pray the seeds of our pain, sown in tears, will produce a great harvest as God puts to use what he puts us through.

I am thankful for my wife, Jennie, who is the most extraordinary person I have ever met. She is velvet-coated steel. If you look up Proverbs 31 in the dictionary, you will find her picture. She has no fear of winter, for her house is clothed in scarlet. I love you, Jennie, and I am thankful we are populating the earth with little women who will become Lion-Puppies just like you.

Alivia, Lenya, Daisy, and Clover, being your daddy and footwasher is the honor of a lifetime. You girls are the head and not the tail. You are so heavenly minded; I am constantly challenged and inspired by you. Thank you for putting up with me during writing days and preaching days and always being my cheerleaders. I love being the minority in this sorority. Bang-Bang-Choo-Choo Train.

Thank you, Trammels and Guidos, for being there on the darkest, coldest night of our winter. Especially you, Coy. You are a rock. For your presence and love we will always be thankful.

To our family (Luskos and Yaps) and those who might as well be family (I'm definitely talking about you, Carrie Rowe), whose love for Lenya is wild and fierce—strength and honor. Heidi and Chelsea, thank you for all the away games and slumber parties with the girls. To the Lauries, thank you for the slipstream your grief gave us. Your footprints in the snow gave us an immeasurable advantage. Carl and Laura Lentz, thank you for being in our corner. Heitzigs and Garcias, you mean so much to us.

To all the Fresh Lifers who have limped through this with us and taken our pain personally, we love you like blood. Heart and soul. Let's run with horses to the end. Wherever we put the soles of our feet, he will prosper us.

Kelli and the whole Trontel tribe, thank you for your friendship and for capturing our life and ministry through the lens of your camera. You have given us a priceless treasure. Amanda Minatra, thank you for being half of Blairnatra and for capturing the photo of Lenya Lion at the Rockstar Gala that is on the cover of this book.

Thank you, Austin and everyone at Wolgemuth & Associates. I have loved being on this ride with you. To Debbie and the W team, thanks for taking a shot on a greenhorn. Thank you for believing in this story and the message burning on my heart and for loving Lenya Lion without knowing her. Meaghan and Debbie, here's to the day we emailed forty-two times about whether you are really seeing stars if you can't perceive them. #HypotheticalObjector

Gregg and Yvonne Esakoff, thank you for letting me use your cabin. I wrote this book in ten states, three different countries, and on a lot of airplanes, but the days overlooking the lake from your deck were my favorites.

To every reader, every podcast listener, every Instagram commenter, and those who have tweeted your love, prayers, and support for our ministry and family—thank you, thank you, thank you. Walt Whitman said that to have great poets, there must be great audiences.

Most of all—thank you Jesus, *the* Lion of the Tribe of Judah. Thank you for turning off the dark, anchoring our souls, opening our eyes, and winching us home.

Finally, to all the hurting hearts and to all those who groan—Saturday can't last forever.

NOTES

Chapter 1: Destined for Impact

1. Randy Lewis, "Tom Petty and the Heartbreakers' Stolen Guitars Recovered," Pop and Hiss: The *L.A. Times* Music Blog, April 17, 2012, http://latimesblogs.latimes.com/music_blog/2012/04/tom-petty-guitars-stolen-theft-recover-heartbreakers.html.
2. "Loki's Arrival," *The Avengers*, directed by Joss Whedon (2012; Burbank, CA: Walt Disney Studios Home Entertainment, 2012), DVD.

Chapter 2: Cows Die There

1. Corrie Ten Boom, *The Hiding Place*, 35th anniversary ed. (Grand Rapids: Baker, 2006), 227.
2. C. H. Spurgeon, *Lectures to My Students* (Grand Rapids: Zondervan, 1954), 26–27.

Chapter 3: The Christmas from Hell

1. C. S. Lewis, *The Silver Chair* (1953; repr. New York: HarperCollins, 2002), 19.

Chapter 4: Turn Off the Dark

1. Meghan Hoyer and Brad Heath, "Mass Killings Occur in USA Once Every Two Weeks," *USA Today*, December 2, 2013, http://

www.usatoday.com/story/news/nation/2012/12/18/mass-killings-common/1778303/.

2. Tara Parker-Pope, "Suicide Rates Rise Sharply in U.S.," *New York Times*, May 2, 2013, http://www.nytimes.com/2013/05/03/health/suicide-rate-rises-sharply-in-us.html?_r=0.
3. M. R. Vincent, *Word Studies in the New Testament*, vol. 3 (New York: Charles Scribner's Sons, 1887), 441; John MacArthur, "Model Spiritual Servants, Part 3: Epaphroditus," Grace to You, https://www.gty.org/resources/print/sermons/50–26.
4. Elisabeth Kübler-Ross, MD, *On Death and Dying: What the Dying Have to Teach Doctors, Nurses, Clergy, and Their Own Families* (New York: Scribner, 1969).
5. K. O. Gangel, *Acts*, vol. 5 (Nashville: Broadman & Holman, 1998), 234–35.
6. Timothy Keller, *The Grieving Sisters*, Encounters with Jesus 3, Kindle ed. (New York: Penguin, 2013), loc 189–91; A. T. Robertson, *Word Pictures in the New Testament* (Nashville: Broadman, 1933), John 11:33.
7. "Turn Off the Dark—Fresh Life Christmas 2012," Vimeo video, from a presentation by Fresh Life Church, Whitefish Performing Arts Center, Whitefish, MT, December 24, 2012, posted by "flc," December 25, 2012, http://vimeo.com/56298156.
8. Reed Kelly, tweet posted March 23, 2014, by @thereedkelly.

Chapter 5: No Inhalers in Heaven

1. Andy Green, "Stephen King: The *Rolling Stone* Interview," *Rolling Stone*, October 31, 2014, http://www.rollingstone.com/culture/features/stephen-king-the-rolling-stone-interview-20141031.
2. C. H. Spurgeon, "The Tent Dissolved and the Mansion Entered" (sermon, May 6, 1883, Metropolitan Tabernacle, Newington, London, England), *Spurgeon's Sermons*, vol. 29, http://www.ccel.org/ccel/spurgeon/sermons29.txt.
3. Brian Campbell and Lawrence A. Tritle, *The Oxford Handbook of Warfare in the Classical World* (New York: Oxford University Press, 2013), 138.

4. Erwin Lutzer, *The Vanishing Power of Death: Conquering Your Greatest Fear* (Chicago: Moody, 2004), 17.

Chapter 6: Cue the Eagle

1. "'Give Me Faith'—Elevation Worship," YouTube video, 7:03, from a worship service at Elevation Church, Charlotte, NC, July 15, 2010, posted by "elevationworship," October 1, 2010, https://www.youtube.com/watch?v=n_Voi3JM8ZA.

Chapter 7: There's No Such Thing as a Wireless Anchor

1. "Lenya Avery:: Celebration of Life," Vimeo video, from a service by Fresh Life Church, Liberty Theater, Kalispell, MT, December 26, 2012, posted by "Levi Lusko," December 27, 2012, http://vimeo.com/56384147.
2. Ross Busby, *Billy Graham: God's Ambassador* (San Diego: Tehabi Books, 1999), 269.
3. "Shoot Straight," *The Hunger Games*, directed by Gary Ross (2012; Santa Monica, CA: Lions Gate Films Home Entertainment, 2012), DVD.
4. Ben Sherwood, *The Survivors Club: The Secrets and Science That Could Change Your Life* (New York: Hachette, 2009), 128.
5. Meg Meeker, MD, *Strong Fathers, Strong Daughters: 10 Secrets Every Father Should Know* (Washington, DC: Regnery, 2006), 189.
6. See notes at Hebrews 6:19–20 in *Nelson* NKJV *Study Bible*, 2nd ed. (Nashville: Thomas Nelson, 2012).
7. "What's His Play?" *The Avengers*, directed by Joss Whedon (2012; Burbank, CA: Walt Disney Studios Home Entertainment, 2012), DVD.
8. Bob Simon, "Free Diving," *60 Minutes*, produced by Michael Gavshon, aired January 13, 2013; transcript and video available at http://www.cbsnews.com/news/death-defying-free-dives-push-boundaries/.
9. Mark Divine, *The Way of the SEAL: Think Like an Elite Warrior* (White Plains, NY: Reader's Digest, 2013), 73.
10. Edward Mote, "My Hope Is Built on Nothing Less," 1834.

Chapter 8: Pain Is a Microphone

1. A. W. Tozer, *The Root of the Righteous* (Harrisburg, PA: Christian Publications, 1955), 137.
2. C. S. Lewis, *The Problem of Pain* (1940; repr. San Francisco: HarperSanFrancisco, 2001), 91.

Chapter 9: Homesickness: An Ache You Can't Shake

1. New York City Department of Health and Mental Hygiene, "Unintentional Drug Poisoning (Overdose) Deaths in New York City, 2000–2012," *Epi Data Brief* (33), September 2013, 1, http://www.nyc.gov/html/doh/downloads/pdf/epi/databrief33.pdf.
2. Kevin Johnson, "Heroin a Growing Threat Across USA, Police Say," *USA Today*, April 17, 2014, http://www.usatoday.com/story/news/nation/2014/04/16/heroin-overdose-addiction-threat/7785549/.
3. US Department of Justice Drug Enforcement Administration, "National Drug Threat Assessment Summary 2014," DEA-DCT-DIR-002–15, November 2014, 9, http://www.dea.gov/resource-center/dir-ndta-unclass.pdf.
4. "DrugFacts: Heroin," National Institute on Drug Abuse, October 2014, http://www.drugabuse.gov/publications/drugfacts/heroin.
5. David Amsden, "The New Face of Heroin," *Rolling Stone*, April 3, 2014, http://www.rollingstone.com/culture/news/the-new-face-of-heroin-20140403.
6. Ken Garfield, *Billy Graham: A Life in Pictures* (Chicago: Triumph Books, 2013), 20.
7. *Wreck-It Ralph*, directed by Rich Moore (2012; Burbank, CA: Walt Disney Studios Home Entertainment, 2013), DVD.
8. The J. B. Phillips translation of the Bible renders the words "on tiptoe." See also A. T. Robertson, Word Pictures in the New Testament (Nashville: Broadman, 1933), Romans 8:19.
9. C. S. Lewis, *The Last Battle* (1956; repr. New York: HarperCollins, 2002), 228.

Chapter 10: Panem et Circenses

1. Juvenal, *Satire*, 10.81.
2. Matthew Bunson, *A Dictionary of the Roman Empire* (New York: Oxford University Press, 1995), 246.
3. Meg Meeker, MD, *Strong Fathers, Strong Daughters: 10 Secrets Every Father Should Know* (Washington, DC: Regnery, 2006), 60.
4. Space Telescope Science Institute, "Hubble Essentials: Quick Facts," HubbleSite, http://hubblesite.org/the_telescope/hubble_essentials/quick_facts.php.
5. Space Telescope Science Institute, "Hubble Essentials," HubbleSite, http://hubblesite.org/the_telescope/hubble_essentials/.
6. Helen H. Lemmel, "Turn Your Eyes upon Jesus," 1922.
7. Edward M. Bounds, *Heaven: A Place, a City, a Home* (London: Fleming H. Revell, 1921), 125.
8. Justin Huggler, "Waiting to Die: Last Days of the Cross-Bred Lions Too Weak to Eat," *Independent*, September 18, 2006, http://www.independent.co.uk/news/world/asia/waiting-to-die-last-days-of-the-crossbred-lions-too-weak-to-eat-416456.html.
9. Palash Kumar, "Lions Dying in Indian Zoo After Failed Experiment," Reuters, September 6, 2006, http://bigcatrescue.org/lions-dying-in-indian-zoo-after-failed-experiment/.

Chapter 11: Run Toward the Roar

1. "Are You Ready for War," *Braveheart*, directed by Mel Gibson (1995; Hollywood: Paramount Home Video, 2002), DVD.
2. Jackson Truax, "Frozen Composers Robert Lopez and Kristen Anderson-Lopez," Awards Daily, November 27, 2013, http://www.awardsdaily.com/blog/2013/11/frozen-composers-robert-lopez-and-kristen-anderson-lopez/; Carly Mallenbaum, "Songwriter: 'Frozen' Was Rewritten for the Song 'Let It Go,'" *USA Today*, March 1, 2014, http://www.usatoday.com/story/life/movies/2014/03/01/frozen-let-it-go/5922623/.
3. "Wow! Ray Finkle's House," *Ace Ventura: Pet Detective*, directed by Tom Shadyac (1994; Burbank, CA: Warner Home Video, 1999), DVD.

Chapter 12: Pencils Down

1. *Online Etymology Dictionary*, s. v. "deadline," http://www.etymonline.com/index.php?term=deadline.
2. Andrew Bonar, *Robert Murray McCheyne* (London: Banner of Truth, 1960).
3. Francis Bret Harte, *Bret Harte's Poems: Complete Edition* (London: George Routledge & Sons, n.d.), 175.
4. Frank G. Allen, "Plus Ultra vs. Ne Plus Ultra," *Autobiography of Frank G. Allen, Minister of the Gospel, and Selections from His Writings*, ed. Robert Graham (Cincinnati: The Guide Printing & Publishing Co, 1887), available at http://biblehub.com/library/allen/autobiography_of_frank_g_allen_minister_of_the_gospel/iii_plus_ultra_vs_ne_plus.htm; Randy Alcorn, *Heaven* (Carol Stream, IL: Tyndale, 2004), 425.
5. These two lines appear in "Only One Life," a poem widely attributed to British missionary C. T. Studd. See Dr. Emerson Eggerichs, *Love and Respect in the Family* (Nashville: Thomas Nelson, 2013), 263.
6. Amy Carmichael, quoted in Joni Eareckson Tada, *Heaven: Your Real Home* (Grand Rapids: Zondervan, 1995), 195.
7. "Far From Home (Main Title)," *Gladiator*, directed by Ridley Scott (2000; Universal City, CA: DreamWorks Home Entertainment, 2000), DVD.

About the Author

Photo: Kelli Trontel

Levi Lusko is the pastor of Fresh Life Church, a multisite church in Montana, and the founder of Skull Church and the O2 Experience. He serves as host for Greg Laurie's Harvest Crusades and travels internationally to speak at churches and conferences. He takes pleasure in small things, like black coffee, new shoes, and fast Internet. He and his wife, Jennie, have four daughters: Alivia, Daisy, Clover, and Lenya, who is in heaven.